Theater Games
for the Lone Actor

Theater Games
for THE
LONE
ACTOR

Viola
Spolin

EDITED BY PAUL AND CAROL SILLS

NORTHWESTERN UNIVERSITY PRESS
EVANSTON, ILLINOIS

Northwestern University Press
Evanston, Illinois 60208-4210

Printed in the United States of America

10 9 8 7 6 5 4 3 2 1

ISBN 0-8101-4010-1

Library of Congress Cataloging-in-Publication Data

Spolin, Viola.
    Theater games for the lone actor / Viola Spolin ; edited
by Paul and Carol Sills with a foreword by Paul Sills.
        p. cm.
    ISBN 0-8101-4010-1 (pbk. : alk. paper)
    1. Improvisation (Acting) 2. Acting. 3. Games. I. Sills,
Carol. II. Sills, Paul. III. Title.
    PN2071.I5 S63 2001
    792'.028—dc21

                                    2001001965

CONTENTS

Glossaries

FOREWORD

Theater Games for the Lone Actor, written when she was in her eighties,* is Viola Spolin's testament to actors/players and to those of us who, like actors, hope to find ourselves in the work we do.

Viola knew she was onto something which she had to impart: the essence of the teaching she had received from Neva Boyd. "From 1924 to 1927 as a student in her house, I received from her an extraordinary training in the use of games, story-telling, folk dance, and dramatics as tools for stimulating creative expression in both children and adults through self-discovery and personal experiencing. The effects of her inspiration never left me for a single day."† As she put it, she had been given the "message to Garcia" and had been entrusted to deliver it through all doubt and danger. In the old

---

* Viola wrote *Theater Games for the Lone Actor* at the request of her publisher and the encouragement of actor/student friends Patricia and Richard Herd and Gary Schwartz, who worked on the first draft under Viola's direction, assisted by her husband, Robert Kolmus Greene.

† Viola Spolin, *Improvisation for the Theater,* 3rd ed. (Evanston, Ill.: Northwestern University Press, 1999), acknowledgments. Miss Boyd founded the Recreational Training School at Chicago's Hull House and served as a professor of group work on the faculty of Northwestern University.

story from the Spanish-American War (1895–98), a lone soldier succeeded in taking a message behind enemy lines to Garcia, the rebel leader, known only to be somewhere on the island of Cuba.*

Viola delivered her message in *Improvisation for the Theater* and the books that followed.† In *Theater Games for the Lone Actor*, she is heightening the message. One must enter present time to encounter one's real, natural self, even though, as she states in her poem "Crystal Ball," "Present time / like the divine / is most difficult / to find." But Viola does show us a way to find it. In this book she declares one can and *must* side coach oneself into the direct experience of playing. "Side coaching is a necessary message to alert your total organism, your whole self, to keep you in process and in present time" (see page 7).

In 1990 Viola said, "Do not think of present time as clock time but rather as a timeless moment, when all are mutually engaged in experiencing and experience, the outcome of which is as yet unknown. You're right there; you're connected and

---

* Elbert Hubbard, "A Message to Garcia," in his magazine *The Philistine* (February 1899). When Viola, born in 1907, was a child, the story was widely told.

† *The Theater Game File, Theater Games for Rehearsal: A Director's Handbook*, and *Theater Games for the Classroom*, all published by Northwestern University Press.

you don't know what's going to happen and that's where the spontaneity is, and that's where the joy is, and that's where the happiness is and that's the everlasting, the never-ending spiral."*

Years earlier, in an unpublished note, she wrote, "Present time is the moment time and space meet—when the ball is in the air." She often said, "Keep your eye on the ball!" This is a metaphor for all of Viola's side coaching.

Side coaching yourself into present time is the very thing you can do that allows you to enter theater space, "*connected, right there*." Understand? You are being given the message to Garcia.

Paul Sills, 2001

---

* From Lisa Law's film *Flashing on the Sixties* (1991).

CRYSTAL BALL

To the witch she did go
to find out what the future holds
and to the seeker the following was told:
    Present time you must find
    and within it dwell,
    for in there is the key
    that opens the door to the great mystery
    and the future you will see.
    But hark!
    If in present time
    you cannot dwell
    you'll have no future to foretell.
    Trapped in the past you'll always be.
So she went forth
to dwell in present time.
But alas!
Present time
like the divine
is most difficult
to find.

AUTHOR'S PREFACE

The Lone Actor

In this handbook of theater games for the solo player, you will learn to enter present time, no matter what is going on around you, through a direct *right now!* experience. Present time as used here is not clock time. It is a moment of full consciousness, awareness, continuous time, a timeless moment (whether seconds, minutes, or hours) with all of your responses awake and alert, ready to guide you and come to your aid, free of past *do's and don'ts, should I or shouldn't I's.*

In present time a path is opened to your intuition, closing the gap between thinking and doing, allowing you, the real you, your natural self, to emerge and experience directly and act freely, present to the moment you are present to.

You, the real you, must be seen. There are many facets to your basic persona unknown even to you, that may come forth, appear, and become visible. You, the unique, invisible, unknown, must emerge, be seen, and connect!

Viola Spolin, 1990

Theater Games
for the Lone Actor

PLAYING THE GAMES

INTO YOUR SPACE

The mysterious
magical
creative
comes from beyond
our daily realities
and
will not
or cannot
respond
until you
are in communion
with the as yet
unknown,
your intuition,
your x-area.
The key?
Get out of your head,
into your space
and await
the invisible stranger.

PLAYING THE GAMES

PLAY! A DIRECT EXPERIENCE WILL FREE your intuition in a life moment, *right now!***** Focus†
will replace your conscious control and playing the games will dissolve your cover-ups. The focus of the games is based on theatrical conventions so that growth as an actor as well as a person will take place.

Let the playing build up your inner strength, your vast incredible potential. Play, for when you do, blood circulates and energy is released into the space, touching and connecting you with everything in that space. You act spontaneously, entering the area of the unexpected, free of the expectations of others. Play with others—fellow players, colleagues,

---

* In the traditional game Tag, for instance, the moment you tag or are tagged by a fellow player is a moment of direct experience.

† The rules of a game are its focus.

family and friends, and whenever you go forth, bring the focus of play along with you!

Viola Spolin, 1992

SIDE COACHING
YOURSELF

WHEN I PLAYED SOFTBALL AS A YOUNG girl on the playground, side coaching was always furnished for a hitter (runner) who was on first base. The side coach acted as another support with a detached overview.

Side coaching is a guide, a directive, a support, a catalyst, a higher view, an inner voice, an extended hand, you might say, given during the playing of a game to help you stay on focus. Side coaching is a necessary message to alert your total organism, your whole self, to keep you in process and in present time, while releasing spontaneity, hidden wisdom, and intuition. Playing and becoming familiar with this work, you will find that your natural creative ability can handle incoming data, knowing what is happening and what side coaching is needed to help you. You will discover that being your own side coach instructs and puts all of you, inside and out, within the direct experience that is taking place, witness to exactly what is going on.

Your effort as your own side coach must be to find and keep yourself—the player—on focus, *out of the head and into the space!* If you have disconnected, you may feel alone, but you, lone actor, are not alone if you *let the space support you!* Be your own diagnostician, objectively recognizing the state you are in, applying the necessary, recommended, side coaching. For instance, when you become aware of and recognize that you are in the grip of fear, avoid trying to find out why (you probably couldn't anyway, as most fear is tied in with past experience and conditioning). Recognize the physical manifestations of fear, the symptoms, you might say, and side coach yourself out of the fear pattern: *Take a ride on your own body!* No analysis, no *if only's. Act!* on the present-time emotional condition.

The whole effort of this work is to bring you, the individual player, close to or back to your own persona, own ground of being, resources, treasure house, intuition, x-area, fresh, open, alive! Seeing the *right now!* state you are in allows you to choose what to do about it. As you become familiar with the games and side coaching, you will have many choices,* whether you find yourself deep in the approval/disapproval syndrome (see page 109) or recognize your ego-centeredness at work. Side coaching, the application of procedures in this book, is not a system of stage behavior but a means of release from the ties that keep you emotionally dependent on outside opinions. *Slow Motion!* or *See unlabeled!* do not give techniques on how to perform, but open up the space around you.

* Side-coaching phrases appear with most games and also in the "Glossary of Side-Coaching Phrases," page 181, with meanings attached. "Suggested Games for Specific Needs" appears on page 123.

BASIC WARM-UP EXERCISE

FOCUS

On the side coaching.

DESCRIPTION

Sit quietly, open to the side coaching. Repeat the exercise two or three times.

SIDE COACHING

Feel yourself sitting in the chair!
Feel the space all around you! Now let the
    space feel you!
Roll your head around! (Let the weight of your
    head do the moving.)
Shoulders at ease! You stay out of it!
Let your head roll to the left and move your
    eyes to the left as far as you can!
Send your sight even farther left! Now roll your
    head to the right!
Move your sight as far to the right as possible!
    Return head to center!
Drop head forward on chest, moving eyes
    downward with your head.

Raise head and let your sight roll back with your
  head as far as possible.
Send your sight back even farther! Return your
  gaze to the center.

FEELING SELF WITH SELF

This exercise, which gives a full-body perception of self, may be used frequently, by itself or leading into a SPACE WALK, pages 17 and 20.

FOCUS

On feeling self with self.

DESCRIPTION

Sit quietly. Physically feel what is against your body as side coached. Side coach continuously. If necessary, coach yourself to keep your eyes open.

SIDE COACHING

Feel your self with your self! Feel your feet with your feet!

Feel your feet inside your stockings and feel your stockings on your feet!

Feel your slacks (or skirt) on your legs and your legs in your slacks or skirt!

Feel your underclothing next to your body and let your body feel your underclothing!

Feel your shirt against your chest and your chest
   against your shirt!
Feel your ring on your finger and your finger in
   your ring!
Feel the hair on your head! Your eyebrows on
   your forehead!
Feel your nose against your cheeks! Feel your
   ears!
Your tongue inside your mouth!
Try to feel the inside of your head with your
   head!
Feel all the space around you! Now let the
   space feel you!

EVALUATION

Was there a difference between feeling your ring
on your finger and feeling your finger in the ring?

SIT IN SILENCE

FOCUS

On silence.

DESCRIPTION

Sit in silence, without subvocal or unspoken thoughts or words.

EVALUATION

Was I able to sit without intrusion from inner or outer distractions?

Did objects around me become more visible?

POINT OF OBSERVATION

True silence without subvocal or unspoken thoughts or words creates an openness as the objects in the immediate environment come to life. Reaching out is also reaching in. Deeper personal resources are reached.

EXHALATION

FOCUS

On exhalation.

DESCRIPTION

Sit, doing nothing, thinking nothing, and breathe, focusing on the exhalation. Sit as if your legs grew straight down from your buttocks. Rest hands on your thighs. Allow your body to align itself. Release shoulder tension. Give a slight hissing sound on the exhalation.

EVALUATION

Did you notice a release of tension on the exhalation and hissing?

SPACE SUBSTANCE

THE SPACE WALK AND SPACE SHAPING exercises which follow are ways of perceiving/sensing/experiencing the environment (space) around us as an actual dimension in which all can enter, communicate, live, and be free. Each player becomes a receiving/sending instrument capable of reaching out beyond the physical self and the immediate environment. As water supports and surrounds marine life, space substance surrounds and supports us. Objects made of space substance may be looked upon as thrusts/projections of the (invisible) inner self into the visible world, intuitively perceived/sensed as a manifest phenomenon, *real!* When the invisible (not yet emerged, inside, unknown) becomes visible—seen and perceived—theater magic! This is the fertile ground of the poet, the artist, the seeker.

SPACE WALK I: EXPLORATION

FOCUS

On feeling space with the whole body.

DESCRIPTION

Walk around the room and feel the space around and against you. Physically investigate it as an unknown substance and give it no name.

SIDE COACHING

Move through the substance and make contact with it!

Feel it against your back! Your neck! Feel it with your whole body!

If you tend to use hands only, coach: Let your hands be as one with your body! Move as a single mass! Explore the substance!

Feel it (space) inside your mouth! Along the outside of your body!

Now, let it feel you! Your arms! Your face! Your whole body!

You go through the space and let the space go through you!

Feel your body shape as you go through it!
Go inside your body and feel where there is
     tenseness!
Feel your facial expression on the inside!
Feel inside your spinal chord! Up and down your
     spine!
Feel your inside with your inside! Observe, note,
     take note!
Feel your skeleton moving in space with your
     skeleton! (Avoid seeing a picture of it.)
Feel your skeleton with your skeleton! Allow
     your joints to move freely!
Feel the movement of your spine! Allow your
     body to align itself!
Feel your pelvic bones! Let your head rest on its
     own pedestal!
Feel your skull with your skull! Now . . . put
     space where your cheeks are!
Around your arm bones! Put space between
     each disc of your spinal column!
Put space where your stomach is!

Now . . . feel the outline of your whole body in
   the space!
Feel where the space ends and you begin! Feel
   your own form!
Allow the space substance to flow through you
   and you flow through the space!
Allow your sight to flow through your eyes!
Take a ride on your own body and view the
   scenery around you!

POINTS OF OBSERVATION

1. You don't necessarily have to do all of this exercise in one session, but as you gradually become
   more familiar with the side coaching, you may
   find it possible to do this and more.
2. Repeat this exercise in Slow Motion. See page
   43 for an introduction to Slow Motion.

SPACE WALK II:
SUPPORT AND EFFORT

FOCUS

On letting space support you or holding yourself together as side coached.

DESCRIPTION

Walk around, moving through the space substance, open to the side coaching.

After you are responding to the support of space, coach yourself to *support yourself*.

Then, coach yourself to go back and *let the space support you*. Change back and forth until the difference between letting space support you and holding yourself together is realized. Calling out different parts of the body helps to release muscleholds.

SIDE COACHING

A
____

As you walk, let space support you! Rest on it!
Lean into it! Let it support your head! Your chin!
   Your eyeballs! Your upper lip!

B
____

Now, you are your sole support! As you walk,
   you are holding yourself together!
Your face!
Your arms!
Your whole skeleton!
If you quit holding yourself together you would
   fly into a thousand pieces!
Call out that which you hold rigid.
You are hanging on to your arms!
Your mouth!
Your forehead!
Note what you feel when you are your sole
   support!

C

Now change! Walk through the space and let
  the space support you!
Don't worry about what that means! Your body
  will understand!
Let the space take over where you were
  holding! Note your body feeling!
Let the space support you! Let space support
  your eyes! Your face. Your shoulders.
Your upper lip. You go through the space and
  let the space go through you!
Continue to change back and forth between
  support and effort until you experience the
  difference.

EVALUATION

How did you feel when space was supporting you?
When you were your own support?

POINT OF OBSERVATION

When you lean on space, an expansiveness and
fullness can be felt as you move through the environment. It is as if you already knew the environment would support you if you let it.

SPACE SUBSTANCE: FOR HANDS

FOCUS

On the space substance between the palms of your hands.

DESCRIPTION

Stand with the palms of your hands facing, and focus on the space substance between the palms of your hands. Coach yourself to move hands up/down, close together/far apart, to feel the space material between the palms of your hands and to play with it. Keep your palms always facing.

SIDE COACHING

Focus on the space material between your palms!

Move your hands back and forth! Move hands apart! Up and down! Anywhere!

Feel the space substance between the palms of your hands!

Play with it! Let it thicken if it does!

EVALUATION

Did you let focus on space substance work for you?
Did you imagine the space material or did you
really feel it? Did space material begin to become
thicker for you?

POINTS OF OBSERVATION

1. This exercise will quickly give you an experience of space substance. However, you must in
   time let the partial focus on the palms of your
   hands dissolve in order to feel head-to-toe freedom to play with and respond to this most
   unique "stuff."
2. If you have studied chemistry you will be aware
   that air is a "substance" (oxygen mixed with
   other gases) which does not exist in outer space
   or on worlds like the moon, which have no
   atmosphere.
3. You may play with a partner—your palms facing
   their palms—and play with the space material,
   moving it about, with full-body involvement.
   Focus on the space substance between the four
   cupped palms, side coaching as above.

PHYSICALIZING AN OBJECT

FOCUS

On giving life and movement to an object.

DESCRIPTION

Select an object, animate or inanimate, and handle and use it, communicating the life and movement of this object. If the object is a bowling ball, for example, you must show what happens to the ball after it has left your hands. A few other examples of objects that can be physicalized are a fish, a bird, a pinball machine, a kite, a yo-yo.

SIDE COACHING

Let your whole body show the object's life!
Keep the object in space! See the object! Out of the head!
Show with your feet! Shoulder blades! Elbows!

EVALUATION

Did you physicalize the object? Did you show or tell?

POINT OF OBSERVATION

The distinction between giving life to the object and manipulating the object is subtle. Be careful not to tell yourself How.

BEGIN AND END WITH OBJECTS

FOCUS

On the object.

DESCRIPTION

In this three-part exercise, a player selects a small object, such as a candy bar, and plays with it in the following ways:

PART I

Perform a simple action with the object, such as taking off the paper wrapper and biting into the candy.

PART II

Then repeat all the action, this time calling out *Begin!* each time fresh contact is made with the object and *End!* when each detail is completed. Coach yourself to do this with great bursts of energy. If done correctly, each detail will be like an individual no-motion frame within a strip of movie film. For example:

SIDE COACHING
Touch candy bar: Begin!
Grasp bar: End! Start to tear the paper: Begin!
 Tear the paper: End!
Ready to toss it away: Begin! Toss it away: End!

PART III

Repeat the action again, this time doing it as *fast* as possible and without calling out *Begin!* and *End!*

SIDE COACHING
Fast! As fast as possible! Double time! Triple time! Faster!

EVALUATION
For part I and part III only: Which part of the exercise was most real for you? Which details came to life (existed in space) for you?

POINTS OF OBSERVATION

1. Part III will be much clearer and sharper than part I, played *out of the head and into the space*, thus visible.

2. Another three-part exercise, BEGIN AND END, page 98, involves bringing a simple Where, Who, and What to life by building each beat within an activity.

WHERE, WHO, AND WHAT

IN IMPROVISATIONAL THEATER, "WHERE," "Who," and "What" (or "WWW") are key terms used in scene work. Knowing Where one is requires relationship with physical objects in a given environment. One shows Who by communicating relationships and behavior. The activity of each character playing in a given environment is called What.

In *Theater Games for the Lone Actor*, for instance, in EMERGING WHERE: PART II, page 38, a player shows Who when contacting the space objects that appear in the chosen Where. Many other theater games in this book use these terms.

PLAYGROUND

FOCUS

On keeping an object (the ball or the jump rope) in space and out of the head.

DESCRIPTION

Play any individual game that requires space objects, such as basketball, jump rope, jacks, pick-up sticks, marbles, and the like. All rules of the chosen game must be followed as you focus your attention on the moving object in space.

SIDE COACHING

Keep it (ball, rope, jacks, etc.) in space!
Give the object its time in space! Play with your whole body!
Keep your eye on the ball!

EVALUATION

Were the objects in space or in your head? Did you have a moment of seeing the object?

POINT OF OBSERVATION

Don't pretend. Imagination or mime will not make the object you are playing with real. When it is in the space, there will be room for it and it will "appear"!

HOW OLD AM I?

FOCUS

On showing the age chosen.

DESCRIPTION

Choose any age. Then, sitting on a chair, which represents a bus-stop bench, focus on showing your age, as in the following two examples:

An adult player begins blowing bubbles with gum, gets it stuck on her nose, cleans the sticky mess with tongue and finger. She fumbles in her pocket for something. Going quickly through her pockets, she pulls out a yo-yo and starts playing with it. The bus arrives; she puts the yo-yo back in her pocket and anxiously fumbles around for bus fare.

An eleven-year-old boy comes onstage in a firm, aggressive manner, holding what seems to be a briefcase, glances down the street, sees nothing, sits down, and opens his briefcase. He thumbs through a few of the sections, pulls out a paper, glances at it, takes a pen out of an inside coat pocket, makes a note on the paper, puts it back into the briefcase. He zips the briefcase closed, looks down the street restlessly—still no bus.

SIDE COACHING

Put the age in the feet! The upper lip! The spine! The bus is half a block away! It's coming closer! It's here!
Sometimes add: It's held up in traffic!

EVALUATION

Did you show or tell? Are age qualities always physical? Are age differences part of an attitude toward life? Did you see the bus or just hear yourself coaching?

POINTS OF OBSERVATION

1. Some players give bodily rhythms and a good deal of activity (business) to help clarify age, which is usually a form of "telling," not showing.
2. Discourage "acting" and "performing" during this exercise by repeating the focus: show the age chosen.
3. After playing this, play NO MOTION WARM-UP, page 61, before playing HOW OLD AM I? REPEAT, which follows.

HOW OLD AM I? REPEAT

FOCUS

On chosen age only.

DESCRIPTION

Choose age and sit quietly, as at a bus stop, repeating the chosen age frequently to yourself. Concentrate on the age only—that is, on the number of years. When age emerges in the body, what is needed for the problem will come up for use. To prepare for action, concentrate on exhalation (see EXHALATION, page 15).

SIDE COACHING

Focus on the exact age! Repeat the number to yourself!
Send the message to the total organism!
When age appears: Bus is a half block away! Bus is held up in traffic!

POINTS OF OBSERVATION

1. The blank mind (free of preconception) is what we are after.

2. This exercise will work if you free your mind of *imagery* relating to the chosen age. Repeating the chosen age over and over in side coaching will help do this.

3. If concentration is truly on age only, you will have a most inspirational experience as your body becomes older or younger spontaneously, with little or no overt action or need for stage business.

4. Concentrating on the age alone serves to release the body to such an extraordinary degree that age may be shown with the minutest movement and gesture, subtleties usually shown by the most accomplished and experienced of actors. One must trust the scheme and let the focus of the exercise do the work.

5. New sources of energy and knowledge may be released. If the problem was solved, you could come from this exercise with more bodily grace evident, with muscular release and shining eyes.

EMERGING WHERE: PART I

FOCUS

On showing/communicating objects that emerge for you in the Where.

DESCRIPTION

Decide on Where. Without preplanning, enter, and by focusing on the Where, physically contact all the objects, touching, hearing, seeing, smelling, *showing* that which emerges in the environment.

SIDE COACHING

Show Where! Contact the object!
See what appears! Use the object! Show Where!
Use the whole stage area!

POINTS OF OBSERVATION

1. Ideally, the object emerges when you enter the Where. At first many will preplan an object, not trusting that one will emerge.
2. When one object is apparent, move on to another.

EMERGING WHERE: PART II

FOCUS

On *showing* each object that emerged in part I and any others that might emerge in the course of playing.

DESCRIPTION

As Who you are playing (the mother, architect, carpenter, or child, for instance), contact and use all the objects that emerged for you in part I, as well as any others that might now emerge.

SIDE COACHING

See the Where! As Who you are, contact every object!
Show Who! Let it emerge! See the object! Show What!
Show! Don't tell! Touch! Smell! Show Where!

EVALUATION

Did you contact each object? Did you feel your character present in the Where? Did you walk through tables or other space objects?

GIBBERISH

GIBBERISH IS THE SUBSTITUTION OF shaped sounds for recognizable words, a vocal utterance accompanying an action, not the translation of a phrase or sentence.

Developing fluency in "no symbol" speech brings with it a release from word patterns that may not come easily to some players. As an introduction to the following games, begin by initiating a simple communication (by yourself, if necessary), such as "What's this?"—"Karoosheeah?" —accompanying the sound with gesture. You might strengthen the gesture and repeat the sound, or utter a new phrase in gibberish. You might tell yourself to sit down ("Moolasay!"), move about ("Rallavo!"), or sing ("Plagee!"), for example.

GIBBERISH/INTRODUCTION

FOCUS

On speaking in gibberish.

DESCRIPTION

Carry on a conversation with yourself (or someone else, whenever possible) in gibberish as if speaking in an unknown language. Converse as if making perfect sense. Communicate in gibberish!

SIDE COACHING

Let the gibberish flow! Communicate!
Use as many sounds as possible! Vary the tone!
Keep your usual speech rhythm!

POINTS OF OBSERVATION

1. Even if you have difficulty speaking in gibberish, don't analyze it; just keep at it. Aim for the flow of sound and body expression to become one.
2. Gibberish helps remove concern and preoccupation with the lines in a script.
3. *Improvisation for the Theater* contains many GIB-BERISH exercises for single players to explore.

GIBBERISH/DEMONSTRATION

FOCUS

On communicating to an audience.

DESCRIPTION

Speaking gibberish, sell or demonstrate something to an audience. If you are alone, play to the rest of the room. When well begun, coach yourself to *repeat*, but this time *pitch* what is being sold or demonstrated.

SIDE COACHING

Sell directly to the audience! Show!
Share the gibberish! Now pitch it! Pitch it
    stronger!

EVALUATION

Was there a difference between selling it and pitching it? Did you *see* or *stare*? Was there variety in the gibberish?

POINTS OF OBSERVATION

1. Pitching the sale should bring about direct

seeing. Pitching, as practiced in carnivals or department stores, requires direct contact with others.

2. You (and your audience, if others are present) will experience the difference when staring becomes seeing. An added depth, a certain quiet, will come into the work when this happens.

SLOW MOTION

SLOW MOTION ALLOWS SPACE TO emerge, to come into existence, to become visible, concrete, and usable. Slow Motion allows objects and people with whom you are in contact to come into focus and be seen, sharply outlined within the same space, giving the depth and life a painter seeks with color.

This space between players gives an opportunity for spoken dialogue to flow, move, travel a distance, creating a dramatic time span, a fruitful pause, an opening to the intuitive and beyond. Slow Motion is much more than moving slowly. It is an energy flow supporting you, a continuous flow of space.

When you first begin to move in Slow Motion, you may simply move slowly with jerky, stop-and-start movements. Side coaching will help bring your whole body into Slow Motion: *"Breathe in*

Slow Motion!" "Blink your eyes in Slow Motion!"
"Reach for the moon in Slow Motion!" In time you
will organically realize the body is in Slow Motion
as in a slow-motion film.

Attaining a true state of Slow Motion has
many, many benefits. The world slows down, placing you in the energy flow—separate from your
censors—dissolving fear and inner ghostly voices,
placing you, the player, seeing, into the total environment.

SLOW/FAST/NORMAL

This four-part exercise will find you playing the same scene at different rates of speed. Keep the playing time of each one fairly short.

PART I

Choose Where, Who, and What—for instance, someone washing the dishes in the kitchen. Play the scene in normal speed until WWW are fairly evident, then stop.

PART II

FOCUS

On repeating the scene in Slow Motion.
Go through the scene again, this time in Slow Motion.

SIDE COACHING

Slow Motion!
Move in Slow Motion!
See in Slow Motion!
The space is moving in Slow Motion!

Think in Slow Motion!
Breathe in Slow Motion!

PART III

FOCUS

On repeating the scene in fast motion.

Redo the action as fast as you can, as in silent movie speedup time, as fast as possible without losing it.

SIDE COACHING

Fast!
As fast as you can!
Keep going as fast as you can!

PART IV

FOCUS

On repeating the scene in normal time.
Now, go back and play the scene in normal rhythms.

EVALUATION

Was there a difference between the first and the last playing? Was there more depth or defined relationship with the WWW in the final time?

POINTS OF OBSERVATION

1. As this exercise allows you to be in a state of play, do not be concerned with exact repetition each time.
2. The final scene, played normal speed, may continue. It may be coached *slow! fast!* or *normal!* By this time the Who is clear, the Where and What assured.
3. SLOW/FAST/NORMAL gives a good shaking up. You can solve the problem of WWW without intellectualizing.

SEEING AND
NOT STARING

STARING IS A CURTAIN IN FRONT OF THE
eyes as surely as when the eyes are closed. It is isolation. When you see even momentarily, observe
how your face and body become more pliant and
natural as muscular tension and fear of contact
disappear. When one player sees another, direct
contact *without attitudes* is the result. Recognition
of another player gives you a glimpse, perhaps, of
yourself.

Those who stare, but do not see, prevent
themselves from directly experiencing their environment and from entering into relation with the
world—the onstage world as well. Know when you
are staring! Know when you are *seeing!* In staring,
you may have your eyes on the other, but your
head is filled with you. In seeing, you enter the
space around you, free of description and information (the past). The following games, through

OCCLUDING, page 102, may help break the habitual holds of staring and enhance *seeing* as a present-time activity.

TOUCH AND BE TOUCHED/ SEE AND BE SEEN

FOCUS

On touching and being touched; on seeing and being seen.

DESCRIPTION

While actually engaged in an activity, alone or with others, or in a SPACE WALK, pages 17 and 20, side coach yourself to *touch and be touched*—by the chair in which you are sitting, the desk you are touching, the hand you may be holding! Coach yourself to *see* a physical object in the room, or another person, and to *allow yourself to be seen!* Avoid pondering; avoid analyzing. Just follow the side coaching.

SIDE COACHING

Touch something!—either on yourself or in the room—and when you truly feel it—let it feel you!

Touch the arm of a chair. Now, let it touch you!

Touch (feel) your cheek. Now let your cheek feel
　　you! Note the difference.
Send your sight out into the environment!
Allow your sight to flow through your eyes!
　　See an object!
The moment you really see it, let the object see
　　you!
Your sight is a physical extension of you!
Allow an object to come in and be seen.
Now let the object see you!

EVALUATION

Did you notice a difference between touching and
being touched? Was there a difference between
seeing an object and letting an object see you? Was
it difficult to allow yourself to be seen?

POINTS OF OBSERVATION

1. This is a valuable exercise which can be played
   even in fleeting moments, helping to create a
   connection between you and your environment.
2. This exercise removes attitudes, information,
   and narration about what you are touching or
   seeing so that a direct experience may occur. It
   can help to maintain freshness in a role.

SEE UNLABELED

FOCUS

On the side coaching.

DESCRIPTION

While sitting and viewing the room, close your eyes. Open them and see the objects in the room without labeling them. Repeat this at least twice, coaching yourself as follows.

SIDE COACHING

See whatever object appears without naming it!
Open your eyes and see! Look up! Look sideways! See unlabeled!
Now, close your eyes again. Open them.
See! See in Slow Motion! See unlabeled!

EVALUATION

Did you notice how fresh your view became, how each object kept its own space (life) when you allowed everything its own space?

POINTS OF OBSERVATION

1. Words are labels. To see without distortion, information, narration, and description allows new insight (and actual sight) to become available.

2. Seeing unlabeled helps you see *through* the eyes, not with them.

3. Play SEE UNLABELED with authority figures, fellow players, friends. You may be amazed at what you see! Because this game avoids information and attitudes about what you are looking at, a fresh new experience is possible.

PERIPHERAL VISION

FOCUS

On extending your vision.

DESCRIPTION

Without turning your head, extend your sight in different directions as coached and then combine those extensions of vision. Repeat this several times and play it frequently.

SIDE COACHING

Turn your eyes to the left as far as possible!
See farther! Even farther! Try to see behind you!
Now turn your eyes to the right as far as you
    can! Circle! See way back!
Now look straight ahead! See right and left at
    the same time!
Try it again: Right! Left! Sight forward! Right/left
    together!
Turn your eyesight to the very back of your
    head!
Bring your eyesight straight forward! Now look
    down as far as your sight can go!

See under your feet! Don't imagine! Try literally
    to do it!
Now look straight forward and up and down at
    the same time! Again!
Now left! Right! Now, straight
    forward/up/down/right/left at the same
    time!

EVALUATION

Was vision extended?

PENETRATION

The following side coaching might be used as a special warm-up, integrated with sense exercises, or used during rehearsal or performance. Also play PENETRATING THE VISIBLE, which follows this game; it is an exercise in penetration involving sight.

FOCUS
On penetrating the environment with your senses.

DESCRIPTION
Think of your sensory equipment as an extended tool. Allow it to move out, extend, cut through, *penetrate!*

SIDE COACHING
Penetrate that color! That taste!
Penetrate that sound! Penetrate that icy chill!
    That fragrance!

PENETRATING THE VISIBLE

FOCUS

On penetrating the environment with sight.

DESCRIPTION

Send your seeing out as a tool to penetrate the environment and return. This exercise involves actively entering visible dimensions through sight. For example, send your sight through a series of windowpanes, out one pane and back through another. Visually explore the objects on the table or the clouds in the sky, and return.

SIDE COACHING

Let your seeing be active! Send your sight out
    as an extension of your eyes!
Let your sight enter that which you see!
    Penetrate that which you see!
Return! Send your sight on another journey!
You are not trying to see! You are at rest!
Your sight is exploring the visible!

POINTS OF OBSERVATION

1. Your sensory equipment (including sight) is a physical extension of *you!*
2. The experience of perception in depth adds dimension to your sight.

NO MOTION

NO MOTION IS A STATE OF QUIET REST (the eye of the storm) where no one has to prove anything. No Motion brings recognition that movement emerges out of no movement, that every seeming nonmovement or nonthought is one complete step, as important as the last and the next, in a step-by-step progression.*

Putting an action or a thought into No Motion helps create change. Peripheral thought, ambivalent thought, are nowhere to be found. No Motion puts thought/action into a simmer, creating vitality, kindling a spark, quieting the physical

---

* See Lao Tzu's *Tao Te Ching*, chapter 26: "The unmoved is the source of all movement" (trans. Stephen Mitchell [New York: HarperCollins, 2000]); "Stillness is the ruler of movement" (trans. James Legge [New York: Dover, 1997]).

equipment (body/brain), bringing energy and new knowledge from deeply hidden sources.*

You might say a halfback who runs across the field is in No Motion, mind in total rest (it certainly should be), free of attitudes, able to see, hear, and thus spontaneously select the route to take, avoiding fellow players who try to obstruct the run and make a tackle.

No Motion does not call for a freeze. It is rather a waiting (not *waiting for*, but *in waiting*). *Take a ride on your own body!* is a side coach that spontaneously evokes a state of being in No Motion. When one takes a ride and doesn't have to drive, there is time to view the scenery. Side coach *No Motion!* whenever it will be useful in your preparation or your work. You may reside in No Motion for a few moments in preparation to playing or during . SPACE WALKS, pages 17 and 20.

---

* This holds for all focus. "Put the focus in No Motion," Viola said. The rule of any game is in No Motion. For instance, when we play Tag, we do not continually remind ourselves to run from "it"—we run, with no time lag. "The pope uses it," Viola said, explaining how he puts names of prospective cardinals in his head and then doesn't worry which will emerge as his choice. The choice is in No Motion.

NO MOTION WARM-UP

FOCUS

On the No Motion within movement.

PART I

DESCRIPTION

Standing in the space, raise your arms, breaking up the flow of movement into a series of stills or frames as on a moving-picture filmstrip. Repeat several times, following your own side coaching and focusing on the No Motion within the movement of your arms.

SIDE COACHING

Raise your arms and lower arms as in a series of stills!

Focus on the feeling of No Motion as you raise your arms!

Focus on doing nothing! Bring your arms down in No Motion!

You stay out of it!

EVALUATION

Can you sense the series of stills your arm movements have left in the space?

PART II

DESCRIPTION

Focusing on the periods (feelings) of No Motion
within the total flow of movement, raise and lower
your arms in regular speed, then triple speed, main-
taining your focus on No Motion, then return to
normal speed. If you feel some muscular tension,
release it, but keep your arms moving, as if floating
on their own.

SIDE COACHING

**Raise your arms in regular speed, focusing on
No Motion!**
**Triple your speed, focusing on No Motion! Up
and down! No Motion!**
**Normal speed in No Motion! No Motion! You
stay out of it!**

EVALUATION

Did you feel that the arms were moving themselves? Did you feel No Motion?
    Did the space thicken?

POINTS OF OBSERVATION

1. This exercise gives a physical feeling and understanding of keeping out of your own way. When you focus on No Motion, your hands, legs, etc., move effortlessly without conscious volition. You are at rest in No Motion—in action without attitude.

2. Practicing No Motion allows one to understand elements of movement.

NO MOTION WALKING

FOCUS

On the No Motion within movement.

DESCRIPTION

Walk around the room, focusing on No Motion within body movement.

SIDE COACHING

Walk around the room in No Motion!

Focus on the periods of No Motion! You do nothing!

Let your body walk around the room! You stay in No Motion!

As you walk, let your sight go out into the whole room and see all the objects around you! Continue.

Let your body walk in No Motion!

Continue. Release any muscular tension!

Take a ride on your body and view the scenery around you!

EVALUATION

Did you begin to get the feeling of yourself doing nothing? Of the body moving itself?

POINTS OF OBSERVATION

1. Exploration of body movement occurs with the focus of No Motion within movement.
2. When No Motion is used, it keeps you quiet and off the subject (you). This loss of concern is a release of fear and anxiety and leaves a clear, blank mind through which something new might come forth.

SPEECH AND SOUND

TO ACQUAINT YOURSELF WITH THE PHYS-
iological structure of language, play the following
exercises, devised to bring you a respite from
subjective thought and interpretation: SEEING
THE WORD, page 71; SPELLING, page 73;
DEAF AUDIENCE, page 78; EXTENDED
SOUND, page 67; and VOWELS AND CONSO-
NANTS, page 75.

All have value for the scripted play as well
as for improvisational theater. SINGING DIA-
LOGUE, page 70, will be heightened by first
playing a round of EXTENDED SOUND, which
follows. Extending sound into space and letting it
land in a fellow player brings about communication in the theater.

EXTENDED SOUND

FOCUS

On keeping sound in space and *letting it land*—in a fellow player or in an object or in an audience member.

DESCRIPTION

PART I

With no fellow players: Stand in the middle of a room and send a sound (not a word) to an object in the room and *let it land*. Contact other objects in the space with a sound.

With other players: Stand in the space at a distance from each other, attentive to the focus. One sends a sound to another player, letting it land; the other player then also sends a sound to a fellow player. Continue until each player has contacted all the others.

SIDE COACHING

Send forth the sound! Keep the sound in space!

Let it land! Extend the sound! Keep the body
    upright!
No words! Keep the sound between you (object
    or fellow player)!
Send the sound in Slow Motion! Send it as fast
    as you can! Normal speed! Don't throw it
    away! Let it land! In the object! In a fellow
    player!

PART II

Coach yourself to focus on the sound as above, but
this time send a word and *let it land* in an object or
a fellow player or a member of the audience.

PART III

Now *send a sentence*, keeping focus on extending
sound and *letting it land*.

EVALUATION

Did you keep the sound in the space? Did the
sound land? Did you physically extend the sound?

POINT OF OBSERVATION

This game shows that sound (dialogue) occupies
space. Play EXTENDED SOUND during re-

hearsals of scripted work, sending dialogue into space and letting it land in a fellow player or fellow players.

SINGING DIALOGUE

FOCUS

On extending the sound of dialogue through singing.

DESCRIPTION

Sing all the dialogue of your script, sides, or improvisation. Create a flow of sound. Focus on the extension of sound; *let it land!* Singing permits repetition of words and also elongation of words. Singing must be addressed to your fellow player(s), if any, audience members, or the objects around you.

SIDE COACHING

Sing out the words! Heighten it!
Elongate the word! Repeat the word! Sing with
**   your whole body!**

POINTS OF OBSERVATION

1. The flow of sounds is a bridge to the intuition.
2. Sing your thoughts around your home. A good singing voice is not necessary as this is an exercise in the extension of *sound*.

SEEING THE WORD

FOCUS

On the side coaching while reading aloud.

DESCRIPTION

Read aloud from a script, story, or other material while side coaching yourself to heighten perception of the words. Let your silent side coaching involve your perceptions of sight, sound, touch, taste, and smell. Let it be spontaneous and not necessarily make analytical sense in the context of the scene.

SIDE COACHING

See the color in the scene! Continue to read aloud.

Focus on the sounds! Ask yourself, "How do you feel about what's happening?" Continue to read aloud. See yourself there (in the scene)!

Heighten the color! Is it gray or sunny? Heighten the smells!

Continue to read. What's the weather? See it all!

EVALUATION

Did the scene feel real? Were you able to leave the word and go into the experience? Did you continue to read aloud while silently side coaching?

POINTS OF OBSERVATION

1. As greater perception is awakened by your side coaching, notice at what moment you begin to leave the word and enter the scene. Your speaking voice will become natural, your body will relax, and words will flow out of you.
2. The stimulation of fuller sense perceptions helps to remove artificiality of speech.

SPELLING

FOCUS
On communicating to another player.

DESCRIPTION
Carry on a conversation with a colleague, family member, or friend, spelling the letters of words aloud instead of speaking the words.

SIDE COACHING
See the letters!
Feel the letters in your mouth!
Spell sensually!
Physically see the shape of the letters!

EVALUATION
Was the conversation understood? Did you see the letters? Did you feel them? Did some insights emerge?

POINTS OF OBSERVATION
1. This exercise helps to keep words empty of subject (me/personal history) and what is commonly called meaning (interpretation).

2. SPELLING works on any speech you may be having difficulty with. Coach yourself as above.

VOWELS AND CONSONANTS

FOCUS

On contacting the vowels or consonants in a word as it is spoken or read.

DESCRIPTION

While reading or speaking, focus on either the vowels or the consonants without putting vocal emphasis on them or changing speech patterns. Continuing in your own rhythm, and without changing that rhythm, begin to *see* the vowels and consonants in the words you are reading and/or speaking.

Coach yourself to give vowels and consonants their rightful place in your speech, seeing each in the words you are reading aloud, until you hear yourself reading without vocally emphasizing vowels and consonants.

Notice how the words leap off the page! Notice the pace and life of its own that each letter has!

SIDE COACHING

Vowels! Consonants! Vowels!

Read vowels in Slow Motion! Speak consonants in Slow Motion!

Vowels! Speed up! Consonants! Normal! Slow Motion!

See the vowels or consonants as you are reading or speaking!

EVALUATION

Did you have a sense of making physical contact with the words spoken? Did you hear what you were saying? Did new meaning emerge in the space between vowels and consonants? Did you read or speak in your normal rhythm?

POINTS OF OBSERVATION

1. Vowels and consonants are the physical structure of language. The clarity and fullness of vowels and consonants in speech leave wide-open spaces free of past reference, emotional content, or interpretation, thus allowing new content to come forth from deeper, untouched areas (intuition.)

2. Be aware of vowels and consonants in your everyday speech as well as in your work on monologues or scripts.

3. VOWELS AND CONSONANTS for two or more players may be found in *Improvisation for the Theater*, 3rd ed., page 396.

DEAF AUDIENCE

If you sometimes feel that you are working in a vacuum, try this exercise.

FOCUS

On communicating a scene or telling a story to a deaf audience.

DESCRIPTION

Go through a scene, using dialogue and action, or tell a story as if those present were deaf to your words. Side coach yourself to *physicalize* your involvement with Where, Who, and What.

SIDE COACHING

Communicate! Physicalize!
Show! Don't Tell!

EVALUATION

Did your work have animation? Could you have physicalized the scene more? Did you keep the physicalizing subtle?

POINTS OF OBSERVATION

1. DEAF AUDIENCE helps to develop physical (kinesthetic) communication.
2. The deaf audience could be a fellow player, director, or casting director.

PHYSICALIZING ATTITUDES

THE FOLLOWING TWO-PART EXERCISES, ATTITUDES: YOUR OWN and ATTITUDES: OTHERS', are lead-ins to HOLD IT, page 88.

ATTITUDES: YOUR OWN

PART I

FOCUS

On feeling and heightening the attitudes present in your face and body.

DESCRIPTION

As you walk around a room, coach yourself to physically *feel* the attitudes present in your face and body, and then to *heighten* the feeling.

SIDE COACHING

Focus on your face!
Feel your face on the inside from the inside!
Feel your tongue! Your jaw! Your nose!
Feel the inside of your nose from the inside!
Now, whatever you feel on the inside of your face, heighten it!
Heighten it!
Now feel your body from the inside! Feel the position of your head!

Allow your body to align itself! Feel how your
 body moves!
Heighten it!

PART II

FOCUS

On feeling and heightening, then holding and
releasing attitudes present in your face and body.

DESCRIPTION

In addition to coaching yourself to feel and to
heighten feeling, coach yourself to *hold* the feeling
and then *release* it, and finally (when you can't
hold the expression any longer) to look at yourself
in a mirror and release the expression.

SIDE COACHING

Hold your tongue from the inside! Hold it!
 Release!
Hold your jaw! Hold it! Release!
Hold your body together! Release! Feel where
 you are tight! Release!
Feel where the inside of your face is dead!
 Release it!
Focus on your facial expression! Focus on your
 body expression!

Allow your body/self to be your own self!
Heighten the expression in your face and body!
    Heighten!
Hold that expression! Hold it!
Feel the body and facial expression from the
    inside! Hold it!
Now look at yourself in a mirror! Release the
    expression!

EVALUATION

Did the expression change when you released it?
What was the attitude? Were you surprised by
what you saw? Is it possible to see yourself as others
see you?

POINT OF OBSERVATION

Stay away from the mirror until you can't hold
your expression any longer. This exercise helps you
gain recognition of when your face and body are in
attitude.

ATTITUDES: OTHERS'

PART I

FOCUS

On physically exploring, heightening, and releasing the facial and body attitudes of others.

DESCRIPTION

As you move about a room, physically pick up a facial or body attitude of someone you know very well. You will be *physically* exploring that person's facial and body attitudes, not *feeling* or *thinking*. After all of the side coaching, look into a mirror and release!

SIDE COACHING

Focus on your face!
Feel your face with the other person's facial
    expression on the inside from the inside!
Whatever you feel on the inside of your face,
    heighten it!
Feel your body as it moves through the space!

Feel your body from the inside! Heighten it!
Feel your body and your face from the inside!
    Heighten it!
Whatever you feel on the inside of your face and
    body, heighten it! Heighten it!
Now release it! Shake up the space! Not your
    body! Shake up the space!

PART II

FOCUS

On physically exploring and heightening, then
holding and releasing the facial and body attitudes
of others.

DESCRIPTION

Again walk around and *physically* pick up a facial
and body attitude of someone you know very well.
The moment you get the physical feeling, *heighten
it!* Follow your side coaching to *hold it!* and to
release it! In the coaching that follows, you will ask
yourself to physicalize two separate people you
know, and you will see that in the second case,
increasing strength is given to the coaching to
heighten! to *hold it!* and to *release!*

SIDE COACHING

Heighten the physical feeling! Heighten it!
Of the lips! The eyes! The jaws! The skeleton!
The whole body! Heighten it! Heighten it!
After you heighten it, see if you can get a little
     sense of how that person feels.
Hold it! Hold it! Now, look at yourself in the
     mirror!
Release! Feel your own skeleton! Feel your own
     face from the inside!
Now, pick another person. Pick up the facial and
     body attitude of that person.
Work from the inside! Work physically!
Stay with the physical attitude, not the emotion!
     Heighten it!
One hundred times! Heighten it!
Exaggerate it to a ridiculous height! Work
     physically!
Heighten it! Now take on the feeling, the sense
     of that person!
Hold it! Hold it! Now look in the mirror!
Release!

EVALUATION

Did the person or persons you chose emerge from
your face and body?

POINTS OF OBSERVATION

1. Stay away from the mirror until you can't hold the attitude any longer.
2. Get to know the difference between the feeling (emotion) and the physical expression.

HOLD IT

FOCUS

On holding a facial and bodily expression through the scene you are working on.

DESCRIPTION

Choose for yourself a short statement of attitude, such as "Nobody loves me," "I never met a person I didn't like," "What a bunch of losers," or "This looks like fun." Find a full facial or bodily expression of the chosen phrase, and when that has taken over, hold it throughout the Where, Who, and What of a scene you are working on.

SIDE COACHING

Hold it! Hold it!
Let the attitude affect your chin, eyes, shoulders, mouth, hands, and feet!
Hold it!

EVALUATION

Were the basic expressions of attitude maintained throughout? Did the attitude affect or influence

your activity? Did the attitude affect your relationship with others?

POINT OF OBSERVATION

HOLD IT, which shows how attitudes affect character, appears as a version for several players in
Improvisation for the Theater, 3rd ed., page 239.

ROUNDING-OUT EXERCISES

CAMERA

FOCUS

Full focus and energy on another player.

DESCRIPTION

Coach yourself (*Camera!*) To put full head-to-toe focus (total attention) on another player while continuing activity. When another player does see you and unconsciously becomes *Camera*, think of that as a moment of pause for you.

SIDE COACHING

Camera!

Continue activity!

Camera!

Think of yourself as one large eye from head to toe!

See with your whole body!

See with the back of your head!

Camera!

See with your feet!

EVALUATION

Did you give the other player your total attention?
Did the activity continue? Did you really *see* the
other person?

POINTS OF OBSERVATION

1. A purpose of CAMERA is to remove *you* (ego),
   allowing the new to come in so that you can perceive stage (theatrical) life fully, free of paranoia.
2. In full attention, the whole body is involved in
   seeing. Playing CAMERA should eliminate
   "How am I doing?"
3. Needless to say, if the other player is not aware
   that you are playing CAMERA, you must take
   care that your focus does not cause discomfort.
4. In EMOTION THROUGH CAMERA TECH-
   NIQUES, *Improvisation for the Theater*, 3rd ed.,
   page 228, concentration is on focusing intense
   body energy on the actor being framed.

SHADOWING

FOCUS

On shadowing the Where, Who, and What.

DESCRIPTION

Side coach yourself as though the character you are playing is totally removed from yourself, detached. Speak aloud or subvocally about the Where, Who, and What. Speak of yourself in the third person, as in the side-coaching examples given.

SIDE COACHING

"She/he realizes the rug needs sweeping."
"She/he pulls the window shades halfway down."
"She/he sees that the evening sunlight is on the table."
"She/he has a moment of elation, knowing that the house will soon be full of laughter."
"She/he straightens the lace tablecloth and brings the empty punch bowl from the sideboard and puts it on the table."
"She/he admires the old cut-glass punch bowl."

EVALUATION

Were you able to see what you were speaking of?
Did you see yourself objectively as the character?

POINTS OF OBSERVATION

1. Shadowing your character creates artistic detachment in yourself.
2. In rehearsal or in performance, focusing on silently shadowing the self often brings an obvious detachment.
3. VERBALIZING THE WHERE, *Improvisation for the Theater*, 3rd ed., page 118, is another exercise in bringing the environment to life.

WHAT'S BEYOND? ENTERING

FOCUS

On What you were doing just before the scene.

DESCRIPTION

Communicate Where you (a character, Who) have been and What you were doing with Whom, if anyone. If you have a script, you know these things; if improvising, let your inner self decide: a fight, a loving encounter, a sick child, for example. Just before "action" is called, or just before your stage entrance, coach yourself as follows.

SIDE COACHING

Reflect What happened in the place you have just come from!

Let your body reflect What just took place! Show it in your shoulders!

Your walk! Your fingertips! Show! Don't tell!

EVALUATION

Did your entrance have full involvement with What happened *beyond?* Did your entrance reflect the Where, Who, and What you were coming from?

WHAT'S BEYOND? EXITING

FOCUS

On What will happen just after the scene.

DESCRIPTION

Communicate Where you (the character) are going, What you will be doing, and with Whom (if anyone): your girlfriend, your boss, the police department, for instance. Just before you exit, coach yourself as follows.

SIDE COACHING

Let your body reflect What is going to happen!
Show! Don't tell!
Reflect the encounter you are going to!
Show it in your neck! Your arms! Your fingers!
    Your toes!
Focus on What or Who you will see!

EVALUATION

Did your exit have full involvement with What may happen *beyond?* Did your exit reflect the Where, Who, and What?

BEGIN AND END

Like BEGIN AND END WITH OBJECTS, page 27, this is a three-part exercise.

PART I

FOCUS
On Where, Who, and What.

DESCRIPTION
Set up a very simple Where, Who, and What. Then enter and play.

For example: Player enters, looks around to make certain no one has seen the entrance, and is obviously about to do something that shouldn't be done. Looks around room. Spots dresser. Goes to dresser. Opens a couple of drawers and riffles the clothes. Runs back to door to make sure no one is coming. Goes through a couple more drawers, finally finding what is sought. Puts it into coat pocket. Takes a quick look in mirror, checking appearance. Leaves through door.

PART II

FOCUS

On recognition of building each beat within an activity (*Begin!* and *End!*).

DESCRIPTION

Now break the scene into a series of smaller scenes, or *beats*. Each *beat*, or smaller scene, is to have its own beginning and end. Call out *Begin!* at the beginning of each beat and *End!* when it ends. Build or intensify each beat/scene one upon the other.*

For example: Player enters (*Begin!*), stands looking around to make sure no one is there, and finally closes door (*End!*). (*Begin!*) Stands and visually scans the room, spots dresser, and goes to it (*End!*). (*Begin!*) Opens a couple of drawers, riffles contents, thinks a noise is heard, quickly shuts drawers, and returns to door to listen (*End!*). (*Begin!*) Glances back at dresser, goes to it again (*End!*). (*Begin!*) Opens more drawers, finds object (*End!*). (*Begin!*) Looks at object in hand, puts it in pocket (*End!*). (*Begin!*) Looks in mirror, straightens coat, and walks out of room (*End!*).

---

* Using the image of walking up the stairs should clarify this point.

SIDE COACHING

Begin! End! Begin!

Give the new beat more energy! End! Build the next beat higher!

Hit the Begin harder (vocally)! Hit the End harder (vocally, physically)!

PART III

FOCUS

On playing the scene as fast as possible, keeping all the details of the scene.

DESCRIPTION

Go through the scene as in part I, without saying *Begin!* and *End!* but doing everything *as fast as possible* while keeping the details of the scene.

SIDE COACHING

Double time! Triple time! Faster!

As fast as possible!

EVALUATION

For part I and part III only: Which scene was most real for you?

POINTS OF OBSERVATION

1. You will usually find that the final scene has more life because the first scene tends to be generalized and the playing subjectively involved, using invention rather than creating. The calling out of *Begin!* and *End!* in part II forces an outside, objective detailing of the objects. The speedup scene, then, profits from the detail created in part II and from the fact that you did not have time to recall the details *Begin!* and *End!* had brought up. You had immediate contact with WWW, present to the present moment.

2. The detail comes through because the static required in *Begin!* and *End!* "holds time" momentarily so that we can *see* an action.

3. For those interested in direction, this exercise provides a detailed breakdown of what must come out of a total scene, giving the single beats within the overall scene and giving knowledge of where one is going. It is equally valuable in improvisational theater, when players are setting scenes for performance.

4. The process of speeding up scenes—without *Begin!* and *End!*—can be employed whenever you wish. It can help to remove generalization and bring a scene to more vivid life.

5. BEGIN AND END reveals an essence, without cerebral (left brain) interference.

OCCLUDING

FOCUS

On occluding the Where, the Who, or the What.

DESCRIPTION

You stay fully with whatever you are side coaching yourself to occlude. Occluding means shutting in or out, but *not ignoring* what you are occluding. Occlude the Where (meaning setting or environment), occlude the Who (meaning character), or occlude the What (meaning activity).

SIDE COACHING

Occlude the Where! Occlude your fellow player(s)!
Occlude the character! Occlude the activity! Occlude the Who!

EVALUATION

Did occluding the Where help you to heighten your relation to a fellow player?

POINTS OF OBSERVATION

1. If you are coached to occlude the Where, your relation (Who) becomes stronger than usual since there is nowhere to turn except to your fellow player.

2. The player, while occluding something, is at the same time embracing it. How can this happen? Like many other games, OCCLUDING is a paradox: the brain tries to figure out how to be aware of that which must be occluded (shut in or shut out.) This produces a magical off-balance moment, one of the gateways into the intuitive. The invisible becomes visible.

3. The player's mind is emptied (freed) of manifestations of attitude or interpretation. This emptying allows energies to flow into and become part of what is *actually* happening.

4. Use OCCLUDING side coaching in SPACE WALKS, pages 17 and 20.

EXITS AND ENTRANCES

FOCUS

On making exits or entrances that fully involve others present.

DESCRIPTION

Present yourself to whomever is present in a room when you enter and when you exit. Repeat as many times as you wish. Each entrance or exit must be so framed that those present are fully involved (connected) with you at that moment. If you barge in or out without such full involvement, *you didn't make it!*

SIDE COACHING

Watch for the moment! Involve yourself!
Don't plan ahead! Play the game! Stay involved!
Out of your head and into the space!

EVALUATION

Which entrances and exits truly had full involvement and which were only attempts at getting attention? Did you stay with what was going on or did you use contrivances, such as tripping, looking sexy, or jumping up and down, which may gain attention but neglect involvement.

POINTS OF OBSERVATION

1. EXITS AND ENTRANCES develops your capacity to become *visible!* Play it at home with family and friends.
2. You may crawl out, dance in, fly out again, or enter with a quiet "hello." No action is barred, no matter how fanciful it may be, as long as it really involves fellow players and comes out of the shared Where, Who, and What.
3. Getting attention is ego-centered, inside your head. Involvement is seeing and using everything outside yourself. *Out of your head and into the space!*

MEMORIZATION

LEARNING LINES SIMULTANEOUSLY WITH fellow players and through the direct experience of stage action is by far the preferred, integrated approach to memorization. Separating dialogue from action is artificial and is reflected in performance. The approach that follows will allow you to absorb the role, which includes the words, that through your own side coaching you will not have learned in isolation.

MEMORIZATION

FOCUS

On the words.

DESCRIPTION

Familiarize yourself with the words in the script while making no conscious attempt to learn them. To begin, *release* as much physical tension as you can. Try a SPACE WALK, pages 17 and 20; EXHALATION, page 15; SIT IN SILENCE, page 14; or *Slow Motion!* page 43. SCORE (page 115) your anxieties or distractions as they come up. Sit in a comfortable chair, lie down, or, if you must move about, pick a pleasant environment.

Sit quietly in No Motion. Decide on nothing. Until you are with your fellow players in the stage life, there is no way you will achieve a full, true, well-developed character. Begin to read. No critiquing, analyzing, interpreting! Just read. *Release!* Stay quiet. Read. *Release!* In the release, let go of your do's and don'ts.

POINTS OF OBSERVATION

1. VOWELS AND CONSONANTS, page 75, will be useful here, and on a second reading, try SEEING THE WORD, page 71.

2. During performance, focus on the action and not the words. *See!* Play CAMERA, page 91. Focused playing allows the action to come through.

FIVE OBSTACLES TO
A DIRECT EXPERIENCE

1. THE APPROVAL/
DISAPPROVAL SYNDROME

If you have survived by trying to please others, fig-uring out what they want you to say and how they want you to act—and then doing so with as much skill and originality as possible, your approval/dis-approval syndrome is highly active. Approval/disapproval received from others has no doubt become your own and, without conscious realiza-tion on your part, is dictating and critiquing the way you do things, creating robotlike behavior in you with almost total loss of any insight. You are not only prevented from having a direct experi-ence, but also blind to what a direct experience is.

The approval/disapproval syndrome will mon-itor behavior if allowed to do so. Watch it working on you when you are having guests for dinner, meeting people, or in a new situation. Observe the roles and cover-ups in you and those around you, shown by attitudes and what comes out of every mouth: hostility, envy, competitiveness, put-downs, resentment, sarcasm, you name it! What we verbalize as our own are the controls that tie and bind, keeping us earthbound and the victim.

2. SELF-PITY

An important ally to the approval/disapproval syndrome is self-pity, which dogs our steps from childhood onward, hiding itself, often disguised by pious statements such as "I won't compromise," "The time was wrong," "It's too much!" "I'll never be able to do it," "He has influential friends," "My family responsibilities won't allow me," "I could never afford it."

Self-pity must be addressed as a separate state of being. Expose it for the debilitating emotion it is. Play SCORE, page 115, and allow self-pity to dissolve.

3. SUCCESS/FAILURE

Success/failure is one of the products of the approval/disapproval syndrome which attacks and inundates us hour after hour, day after day. Rushing to succeed and giving in to and accepting failure drain precious revitalizing energy, weakening our very life force.

If success/failure were not tied to the approval/ disapproval syndrome, failing or succeeding could stand apart, distant from your private heaven or hell, and become a problem to be viewed and handled. You could transcend the severe crippling stigma attached to failing. But since we are culturally obsessed with success, inner ghostly voices (see page 158) from the past complicate the issue, saying "You're a loser," "You'll never make it," and the like.

When you find yourself in the grip of success/ failure, *stop!* Forget that negative is the opposite of positive; that success is the opposite of failure. Transcend opposites! Look, listen, review. Observe what is at hand: *a problem*—which can be solved, or must be lived with or discarded. Being focused on the problem, you will be in a position to accept any outcome. True, you might fail to get a job, might lose a lover, which could be real, sad, even devastating experiences, but if you have a *focus* (see page 157), you will not be engulfed in fear or lose access to your intuition, the energy source needed to solve the problem.

4. ATTITUDES

We live in a culture preoccupied with appearances (status). Attitudes "clog the machine" and play a heavy role in our day-to-day living, keeping us from directly handling a problem.

Consider a cat, who is washing herself when a collar is put on her. Having no attitude about this obstacle, the cat continues to work in the same rhythm. She continues to work on the problem! When you have an obstacle put in your way, don't let an attitude* divert you and prevent you from directly working on the problem.

5. FEAR

Another obstacle that cuts you off from the ongoing event (problem) is *fear*—emotion that is trapped, buried, and hidden in the past. Fear impedes present-time action, stirring up stress, anxiety, and self-pity and producing confusion and self-doubt.

When you find yourself unable to function, feel yourself under scrutiny (a specimen pinned to the board waiting for rejection)—drained, empty, in a void, everything alien, strange, not of your world, your viscera in turmoil, weak, helpless— heart thumping, hands sweating, mouth dry, panicked—everything rushing by in speeded-up

---

* See SPACE WALK/ATTITUDE, part II, *Improvisation for the Theater*, 3rd ed., page 392.

time—in other words, very, very uncomfortable, you are entangled in fear and it has immobilized you. Name the cause!* Know it as fear, which you must overcome, through a direct, *right now!* experience.

DIRECT EXPERIENCE

When you recognize the signs of any of the five obstacles to a direct experience, side coach yourself to *pause!*† Choose a focus and *connect!* Focus on *Slow Motion*,‡ for instance, and watch the room, its contents, objects, and people, and most important *you*, come together in the space. When you are focused, connected, giving full head-to-toe attention to What is going on around you *right now!*—to Where you are, to Who is there (including you)—then you are no longer fragmented and disconnected. Fear dissolves, clearing your head and silencing the interfering approval/disapproval clutter of do's and don'ts. No longer blocked off or

---

* Play SCORE, page 115.

† The pause is seeing what is happening right now! A direct experience, free of the past, giving full attention to what is at hand.

‡ "Slow Motion," page 43; SLOW/FAST/NORMAL, page 45.

cut off from your ground of being, your own true nature (self) emerges, ready for present-time action and interaction.

SCORE

In this exercise you will score (tally) your personal emotions, mannerisms, behavior, habits—without comment, without analysis, without shame or guilt, without justification, without confession, and without intent to change or effort to get rid of the emotion or mannerism. You are not to feel responsible for your emotions or have positive or negative thoughts. Just be responsible for scoring them!

Scoring the feelings which attach to any activity gives you detachment from them and lets them dissolve. Scoring gives you a direct experience.

This game insists that you make your mark somehow. If you can't write a score down, hit the arm of a chair. A direct experience is necessary to help clear you from the hold of the past and is a state of being beyond the power of your negative emotions. Scoring your own behavior and emotions is taking personal responsibility. As in all the games, present time is the goal. It is in present time that the "I" becomes an eye and we see unlabeled.

FOCUS

On acting on a problem as it is taking place.

DESCRIPTION

Observe an emotion and name it. Recognize it, then *act!*—which is to say, *score* it. For example, if you are feeling anxiety, tally it: ANXIETY //// ///.

If the anxiety rises as you tally, score it again. The moment of scoring may be seen as a *pause*. In this pause (rest), you can see what is happening *right now*. If another emotion takes over, then score the new emotion—for instance: FEAR: ///. Out of fear may come panic. Hang on and keep tally until another emotion arrives or panic dissolves and is no more or turns into something else.

FOR SCORING

A mirror works. Use soap for a marker.

A small tablet and pencil or pen work.

Away from suitable equipment, tear off bits of paper and count them when you get home. If all else fails, make a noise, cough, or hit the arm of the chair—anything to make a *pause* to know that you recognize what is going on by *being there*.

POINTS OF OBSERVATION

1. The moments you score, moments to be repeated often again, are direct experiences. In giving full attention to what is at hand, you are briefly free of the past and its opinions, attitudes, and positive/negative emotions.

2. Remember, you are not responsible for your emotions or mannerisms. You are responsible only for *scoring* them. Don't take responsibility, take *note!* Something happens; a door opens.

3. You may be certain that your anxiety and the fear that is venting itself, attached to the ongoing event, have little to do with what is actually happening. Emotions buried in long-past episodes dog every step we take. Forget trying to reason or analyze. There's always a reason! No blame, no confession. Just score your own behavior and emotions, *right now!*

Score Variations

SCORE: BOREDOM

Keep making your mark under the word "boredom" until the simple word along with the feeling of boredom dissolves or you forget the whole matter. If another feeling, emotion, or thought emerges, score *it!*

On Boredom

QUESTION: I'm always bored at parties. What can I do?

ANSWER: Become the life of the party!

QUESTION: My mate never does anything right. What should I do?

ANSWER: Fall in love!

SCORE: EATING

Note anything and everything you pop into your mouth and the time you ate it, whether it is a crumb off the table at 11:15 A.M. or a piece of pie à la mode at 10:30 P.M.

SCORE: OVEREXPLAINING

How often do you hear yourself and others repeat or overexplain the obvious? *Score this!* Observe when subvocally going over your behavior after an event. Keep score until the emergence of an exact feeling. Let emergence take its reluctant time to appear. Keep on the watch for it, and, in the meantime, just score *overexplaining*.

POINT OF OBSERVATION

Down with analyzing, justification, interpretation, and New Year's resolutions! They only clutter your space.

SCORE: REPEATED PHYSICAL MANNERISMS

Write down the mannerism and score it. *Look at it!* The mannerism? No, the score, and watch the mannerism dissolve, like cotton candy, if you stay out of it. Try it. Take a risk! If and when the mannerism returns or another takes its place, keep score on the recurrence.

SCORE: SPECIAL THEME DAYS

Any day you wish, observe just one particular feeling, emotion, type of behavior, habit you indulge in. You are probably aware of one or two that persistently keep coming forward in your daily actions.

1. Isolate one.
2. Choose your time/space for observation.
3. Observe *when* you behave this way, not *why*.

POINTS OF OBSERVATION

1. Explore other common behavior patterns. A few are There's Always a Reason, It's Your Fault, I Can't/Self-Doubt, Being Helpful, Being Right/Being Self-Satisfied, I Wish, I'm Sorry, Bragging, Lies, Who Did You Beat to the Draw Today? Bribery Day, Sour Grapes, Major Headaches, Pass/Fail Day, and If Only!

2. If you are having discomfort with the exercises, and anxiety, for instance, continues to recur, no matter how often you score, just drop it. You will anyway. At the point of dropping it, however, make a note of your state of mind. Remember, this is just between you and you.

3. SCORE exercises are not designed to force you to change. If, by standing aside and taking note of *you*, you clear your space to let some fresh air in, matters will take care of themselves without your interference. Don't change. Don't not change. Just *keep score*.

GOING FORTH

GO FORTH (THE COMET!), KNOWING YOU must get into present time—and play the games—at home, en route, in the casting office, the dressing room, as well as on the stage or the set.

On arrival, take a moment to contact the environment you are in. Trust yourself and coach your playing to see, hear, and relate to fellow players. Lean on the words; be the channel for the words to flow through, to connect the scene, the characters, and you. Allow the playwright's script to speak and play through you! Do your homework well and you could be in one integrated piece—coaching yourself and playing effortlessly when the side-coaching phrases you have learned emerge for your use at the moment you need them.

For the lone actor, onstage and off, in preparation for any number of situations, whether it is an audition or a rehearsal or a performance, one must confront, battle, and meet that which is tied to and tangled with the past; one must enter a moment of full consciousness and get into present time.

Play SCORE, page 115, the exercise in keeping tally of your emotions. A *pause* occurs in SCORE the moment when you know that you know. In the *pause*, seeing what is happening *right now*, free of the past, you give full attention to what is at hand. Full attention might be the flash behind the steering wheel that prevents disaster, a moment of recognition of a world falling apart, or the big-league batter behind a bat. Seeing what is happening *right now!* allows participation.

Preparation for the lone actor, getting into process at home or on the set, requires that you turn your light on—to see Where you are, Who you are, and What you are really doing. It requires that you seek present time, that you make connection with everything around you.

SUGGESTED GAMES
FOR SPECIFIC NEEDS

AT HOME/GETTING READY

SPACE WALK, pages 17 and 20: *Out of your head and into the space!*

SCORE, page 115: *Score!* your panic, anxiety.

Slow Motion! page 43: Coach *Slow Motion!* to seeing, touching, thinking; to everything and everybody.

WORKING ON THE SCRIPT

SEEING THE WORD, page 71: Stimulates fuller sense perceptions, natural speech.

VOWELS AND CONSONANTS, page 75: Cleans speech and allows new content to come forth.

EN ROUTE—ON THE ROAD, IN THE SUBWAY, OR IN THE ELEVATOR

FEELING SELF WITH SELF, page 12: Gives player a full-body perception of self.

PENETRATING THE VISIBLE, page 57: Penetrate the environment through sight.

TOUCH AND BE TOUCHED/SEE AND BE SEEN, page 50: *When you see it, allow it* (an object or a person) *to see you!*

Slow Motion! page 43: See and feel in Slow Motion.

IN THE OFFICE/THEATER/ WAITING ROOM

Slow Motion! page 43: Calms anxiety, puts you in present time.

TOUCH AND BE TOUCHED/SEE AND BE SEEN, page 50: Creates a connection between you and your environment.

SEE UNLABELED, page 52: Stops information, puts you *there in your Where*, in touch with your environment.

THE INTERVIEW/AUDITION

DEAF AUDIENCE, page 78: Focus upon communicating.

CAMERA, page 91: Putting full focus and energy on another.

Slow Motion! page 43: Helps you enter present time; soothes.

ATTITUDES: YOUR OWN, page 81: Coach yourself to *Release!*

IN REHEARSAL AND ON THE SET

SHADOWING, page 93: Detachment from character.

WHAT'S BEYOND? ENTERING, page 95: Focus is on what happened, what you were doing, with whom, just before the scene.

WHAT'S BEYOND? EXITING, page 97: Focus is on what will happen, What you will be doing, with whom, after the scene.

VOWELS AND CONSONANTS, page 75: Allows new content to emerge; physicalizing the written word.

EXITS AND ENTRANCES, page 104: You become visible!

SEE UNLABELED, page 52: To see anew, directly, without information, description, or narration.

No Motion! page 59: Clears the mind of attitudes.

Slow Motion! page 43: Helps you enter present time, allowing others to be seen by you.

HOLD IT, page 88: Brings up characters from your vast personal computer.

TRADITIONAL GAMES

THE TRADITIONAL GAMES CHOSEN FOR this book are meant to be played with others. A theater game workshop session with fellow players usually starts (and often ends) by playing a traditional game, providing joyous interaction and a bridge from the outside world into the spontaneity of theater play. A workshop is a sequence of activities with a theater game or group of theater games at its core. Warm-up traditional games prepare players for the day's offerings of theater games, and wrap-up traditional games, like lead-ins, help focus energies for the next learning experience. When workshop energy flags, the side coach often decides it is time to play a game.

Viola's choice of traditional games usually came from Neva Boyd's *Handbook of Recreational Games.**

---

* Neva L. Boyd, *Handbook of Games* (Chicago: H. T. Fitzsimons, 1945), reprinted as *Handbook of Recreational Games* (New York: Dover, 1975).

Miss Boyd, who was Spolin's inspiring teacher, states in the foreword to her handbook, "The vitality of the game lies in the creative process of playing it." Let us try to hear her teaching:

Because of its dynamic character, the playing of a game is never twice alike.

The discipline of making judgments, often instantaneously, and of acting upon them within a static frame of reference, i.e., the verbalized rules, is unique to the playing of games.

While the game is an imaginatively set up structure into which the players thrust themselves psychologically, they act consistently with the demands of the situation, and thereby subject themselves to self-imposed discipline,* which involves many aspects of social behavior. Games are the organized accumulation of play-behavior, and since play-behavior is centered largely in the thalamic region of the nervous system, therefore closely related to the outside world, every player has access to the stimulation of the

---

*Viola always said, "Discipline is involvement!" See Spolin, *Improvisation for the Theater*, 3rd ed., page xv.

> dynamic process, and of necessity gets values out of his/her own experience. Because this is true, any attempt to set up values as goals for the players would tend to defeat the possibility of their experiencing these values spontaneously.*

It is common knowledge that the spirit of traditional games is rooted in our history and folk life. To quote J. Christian Bay, in his foreword to Boyd's *Folk Games of Denmark and Sweden*, "Every trait in the daily life, diversion and festive display of the people has grown out of centuries of usage. On the whole (these games) express ideals as old as the earth itself and the fundamental thought in the life of any people is to keep the faith of the forebears." These games touch us, in short, where we are most human.

---

* Boyd, *Handbook of Recreational Games*, foreword.

HOW MUCH DO YOU REMEMBER?

FOCUS

On being open both to reading and to hearing.

DESCRIPTION

This game has two players: a reader and a talker. The reader begins to silently read any story or article from a book or magazine while the talker relates some incident directly to the reader.

Before reversing roles, the reader tells the talker what was read and what was heard.

ADDITIONAL MEMORY GAMES

The following three games can be played at home or with a few other players: OBSERVATION GAME, page 130; and THREE CHANGES, page 131.

OBSERVATION GAME

A dozen or more real objects are placed on a tray, which is set in the center of the circle of players. After ten or fifteen seconds, the tray is covered and/or removed. The players then write individual lists of the names of as many of the objects as they can remember. The lists are then compared with the tray of objects.

THREE CHANGES

Full group counts off in teams of two. Each player observes the opposite player and notes dress, hair, etc. Players then turn their backs on one another and each player changes three things on his or her person—parts hair, folds cuff, unties lace, etc.

Players then face each other again and each player identifies what changes the opposite player has made. Ask players to switch partners and make four changes. Continue to change partners after each round of playing. Seven, eight, or even nine changes are possible.

POINT OF OBSERVATION

Do not let players know that you plan to increase the changes until after the first playing. Many are worried how to find three changes. Four or more will create a good deal of excitement. This is an excellent exercise for players, taxing their powers of making do (improvising) on a simple physical level. Players are forced to look at a "barren" land, as it were, and find things to use for the game their eye did not see at first glance. This has been called the Survival Game.

CONCENTRATION

This game is played with a complete deck of cards placed facedown in rows upon the table. The aim is to match the cards in pairs: two fives, two aces, etc. The first player turns up a card, lays it faceup *in its place,* and then turns up another. If they make a pair, the player may take them, turn up two more as described, and continue until unable to make a pair.

The player then turns down the cards *in the order in which they were turned up.* This is done to permit all players to memorize the cards and their positions. The players continue in turn until all the cards are matched. Quiet and concentration are necessary in playing this game. The player who has the most cards when all are picked up wins the game.

GHOST

FOCUS

On not completing the spelling of a word, on penalty of becoming one-third of a ghost.

DESCRIPTION

Players sit in a circle and one calls out the first letter of a word that he or she has in mind but does not disclose. For instance, if the word is "which," "w" is said. The next player, thinking of a word beginning with the letter "w," for instance, "work," says "o." The third player may also think of the word "work," and add "r." The fourth player must avoid saying either "k" or "d," which would complete a word, and think of another letter to follow "r" that will not complete a word, possibly thinking of "worst" and adding "s." The fifth player may be saved by thinking of "worship" and adding "h." The game continues until a player is forced to finish a word, in which case the player becomes one-third of a ghost but goes on playing.

A player who cannot think of a word and has to give up is thereby made one-third of a ghost. The next player continues. Anyone may challenge a player who is suspected of adding a letter without having a word in mind or misspelling a word. If found guilty, that player becomes one-third of a ghost; if not, the accuser becomes one-third of a ghost.

A player who ends a word three times becomes a whole ghost and is then out of the spelling, but tries to get others to chat. If successful, the victim becomes a whole ghost also. The game continues until all but one are ghosts.

WHEN I GO TO CALIFORNIA

Teams of ten to twelve players in a circle.

PART I

The traditional game. First player says, "When I go to California, I'm going to take my kite (or any other object)." Second player says, "When I go to California, I'm going to take my kite and my hat box." Third player takes kite, hat box, and adds something new. Each player takes in *exact order* all that has gone before and adds a new object. Player who makes a mistake is out and the game continues until only one player is left.

PART II

Same team plays as above with a new series of objects, but instead of saying "take my shoes," for example, player *shows* putting on shoes. The next player repeats this action and adds a new object, perhaps showing a flute being played. As in part I, each player repeats all that has gone before and shows a new action nonverbally.

PART III

The game is played again as in part I, with a new series of objects, and this time players take time to *see* each object as they listen.

MY SHIP IS COMING FROM LONDON

This game is played the same way as WHEN I GO TO CALIFORNIA, page 135, except that in this game the articles are named in alphabetical order. For example, the first player may say, "My ship is coming from London laden with apples." The next player repeats this and may add "beans," and so on, until the alphabet is completed. The player who makes a mistake must drop out of the game and does not add an object. The game continues until the last one fails or until the alphabet is completed.

GEOGRAPHY

Players sit in a circle. One begins by naming a city, Denver, for example. The next player must name a city beginning with "r," the letter with which the first player's word ended, thus saying "Rockford," and so on.

Any player who fails to name a city within a reasonable length of time is permanently out of the game. No name may be used more than once, even though there may be many cities of that name. The game continues until only one player remains.

BUZZ

The players are seated in a circle. One player starts the game by saying "One"; the next says "Two"; the counting proceeds around the circle until the number seven is reached, for which the word "buzz" is substituted.

The players continue counting, always substituting "buzz" for any number in which the digit seven occurs, such as seventeen or twenty-seven. "Buzz" is also substituted for any number which is a multiple of seven, such as fourteen or twenty-one. Upon reaching seventy, the counting proceeds as "buzz-one," "buzz-two," etc. Seventy-seven is "buzz-buzz."

The player who says "buzz" in the wrong place, gives a number when he or she should have said "buzz," or calls a wrong number, drops out of the game. Counting continues from where the mistake was made. The game proceeds until all are out.

RHYTHM

Players sit in a circle and establish ¾ (1, 2, 3) rhythmic movement as follows:

1. Pat both hands on lap.
2. Clap hands together.
3. Snap fingers of right hand.

The game begins with one player starting the rhythm and all others joining in. On the third beat this player says "Rhythm" and continues without a break until the following third beat, when he or she gives any letter to the player on the left. This second player, on the following third beat, gives a word beginning with that letter and, on the next third beat, a letter to the player on the left. This third player, in turn, gives a word beginning with that letter, and so on.

RHYTHM continues until a player fails to give a letter or a word on the correct beat or repeats a word given by another player in the course of the game. When such occurs, he or she reestablishes the rhythm and begins the game again.

PROVERBS

One player leaves the room while the others select a proverb, such as "Waste not, want not," "Faint heart never won fair lady," or "Better late than never." The words of the proverb are then distributed among all the players, who sit in a circle. Should there be more players than words, the proverb is repeated until all have a word.

The player who left returns and, beginning with any player, asks a question of each in succession. Each must use his or her word in a sentence, avoiding calling attention to the word. The player whose answer reveals the proverb becomes the next questioner and leaves the room.

RHYMES

The group sits in a circle with one player in the center, who speaks a one-syllable word and points to any other player who must give a word that rhymes with it before the center player counts to ten. A player who fails to give a word within the allotted time must exchange places with the center player; otherwise the center player continues. A player who uses a word once used by another player exchanges places with the center player.

TRANSFORMATION OF WORDS

Players are given pencils and paper and assigned a word to be changed into another word. The process must be that of making a new word by changing one letter at a time in each word that is formed. For example, the word "pine" once changed as follows: pine, pane, pare, pore, pole, poll, pull, pulp.

It is interesting to experiment with words, not knowing whether they can be transformed.

NAME SIX

All the players except one, who stands in the center, sit in a circle. The center player keeps eyes closed while the others pass any small object along from one to another. When the center player claps hands, the player caught with the object must keep it until given a letter of the alphabet by the center player.

Then the seated player must start the object on its way so that it passes through the hands of each player in the circle in turn. By the time it returns, six objects, beginning with the letter given by the center player, must have been named by the player.

If the player does not succeed in naming six objects in the time that the object makes the round of the circle, that player must change places with the one in the center.

If the circle is small, the object can be passed around two and possibly more times.

CRAMBO, OR I'M THINKING OF A WORD

FOCUS

On defining and on rhyming.

DESCRIPTION

The players sit in a circle. The first player says, "I'm thinking of a word that rhymes with 'sing'" (giving out any word that rhymes with the word kept in mind). The player to the left defines a word that rhymes with "sing," asking, for example, "Is it part of the equipment found on most playgrounds?" The first player answers, "No, it is not 'swing.'" Players, in turn, continue to define words that rhyme with "sing," and the first player answers each with, "No, it is not 'fling,' 'king,'" etc., until someone's question defines the word in mind. Then the first player says, "Yes, it is . . ."

If the player had "ring" as worn on one's finger in mind, he or she would say, "No, it is not 'ring,'" if asked by someone "Is it the tolling of a bell?" In other words, the *definition*, not the word, is the determiner. The player who defines the word that the first player has in mind gets the next turn to start the game.

If the first player does not guess the word that has been defined, the player who gave the definition begins the game again with another word.

Proper nouns are not permissible, and the word given by the first player must have the same number of syllables as the word of which he or she is thinking.

GLOSSARIES

VIOLA'S DICTIONARY

Learning the vocabulary of this teaching will help you to make it your own. The following terms are defined with this in mind. If they seem overdefined, it is because they attempt to fit as many frames of reference as possible to spark insights and clarify the intent of theater games.

This closely follows the section "Definition of Terms" that appears in *Improvisation for the Theater*, 3rd ed., page 355. Several specific *Theater Games for the Lone Actor* definitions* have been added and certain original definitions have been slightly expanded or changed† to accord with *Theater Games for the Lone Actor* definitions of terms.

---

* New definitions are included for "cover-up," "inner voice," "off-balance moment," "spontaneous," "subjectivity."

† *Theater Games for the Lone Actor* versions of previous definitions appear for "focus," "ghostly voices," "judging," "pause," "problem," "problem solving," "side coaching," and "Where," "Who," and "What" (WWW).

Act: To make something happen; to move out into the environment; to act upon.

Acting: Avoiding (resisting) focus by hiding behind a character; subjective manipulation of the art form; using character or emotion to avoid contact with the theater reality; mirroring oneself; a wall between players.

Acting Problem: Solving the focus; a problem when solved results in an organic knowledge of the theater technique; a problem which prefigures a solution; developing theater techniques; theater games.

Action: The energy released in working a problem; the play between actors; playing.

Activity: Movement onstage.

Ad-lib: Not to be confused with improvisation; ad-lib is individual cleverness, not evolved dialogue.

Advanced Student: A player who becomes involved in the focus of a game and lets it work for him or her; one who accepts the rules of the game and works to solve the problem; one who keeps the agreed reality alive; one who plays.

Assumption: Not communicating; letting fellow actors or audience detail a generality; letting others do your work; filling in for another player; *Show what you mean! Say what you mean!*

Audience (Individuals): Our guests; the most revered members of the theater; part of the game, not the "lonely looker-inners"; a most important part of theater.

Authoritarianism: Imposing one's own experiences, frames of reference, and behavior patterns upon another; denial of self-experience to another.

Awareness: Sensory involvement with the environment; moving out into the environment.

Beat: A measure; the time between crises; a series of scenes within a scene; can be one moment or ten minutes; "begin and end."

Becoming Audience: Tendency to lose objective reality and begin to judge oneself as one plays a scene; looking out to audience to see if they "like" one's work; watching fellow actors or oneself instead of participating in the scene.

Believing: Something personal to the actor and not necessary to creating stage reality.

Biographies: Information, statistics, background, etc., written about a character in a play in order to provide given categories to assist the actor in playing a role; sometimes useful in formal theater to help the director to gain insight into the actors; should be avoided in improvisational theater, for it prevents spontaneous selection of material and keeps players from an intuitive experience; "No biographies!"

Blocking: Integration of the players, set pieces, sound, and light for the stage picture; clarity of movement for communication; emphasizing character relationship; physicalizing stage life.

Bodily Awareness: Total physical attentiveness to what is happening onstage and in the audience; skill in using all parts of the body (doors can be shut with feet, and a hip can move an object); physicalizing.

Body Memory: Memory retained in the body at the point of past experiences; physical memory as opposed to mind or intellectual retention of past experience; sensory retention of past experiences; muscular attitudes; "Let your body remember!"

Breakthrough: The point at which a student's spontaneity arises to meet a crisis onstage; the moment of letting go resistances and static frames of reference; a moment of seeing things from a different point of view; a moment of insight into the focus; trusting the scheme; the moment of growth.

Character: People; human beings; real people; the physical expression of a person; speaks for himself or herself.

Character Agility: The ability to spontaneously select physical qualities of a chosen character while improvising; ability to use image, color, sound, mood, etc., to locate character qualities.

Characterization: Selecting certain physical mannerisms, tones of voice, rhythm, etc., in order to play a specific character or type of character; giving life to the character through the stage reality.

Communication: Experiencing; the skill of the player in sharing stage reality so the audience can understand; direct experience as opposed to interpretation or assumption.

Conflict: A tug-of-war with one's self or between players calling for some decision; persuasion or goal to be reached; lack of agreement; a device for generating stage energy; an imposed tension and release as opposed to problem (organic).

Contact: Sensory impact; physical and visual involvement with the theater environment (Where, Who, audience, etc.); to touch, see, smell, hear, and look; to know what you touch; communication.

Costume Pieces: Partial costume bits which can be used in creating character; character costume suggestions as opposed to full-dress costumes (a box full of hats).

Cover-up: The real, unique you covered up with a self-protecting armor of attitudes, seductions, lies, deceits, politeness, judgments, and insensitivity. Play, and dig out the real, basic, unique you!

Creation: Create (limited) plus intuit (unlimited) equals creation.

Crisis: A heightened moment ready to change form; theater (playing) is a series of crises; alternative; the peak or breaking point of a static moment or situation where many eventualities are possible; a moment of tension in which the outcome is unknown; the player must be primed to meet any change, simple or extraordinary, the crisis may bring.

Detachment: Involvement with Where, Who, and What (a direct experience); an optimum position; distancing oneself for better viewing (focus). Separation from our ego-centered self allows a relation free of emotional involvement.

Detail: Every object, minute or massive, animate or inanimate, that exists within the stage environment.

Diagnosis: The teacher-director's skill in finding out what problems are needed to solve problems.

Dialogue: Words actors use in talking to one another to implement and build the reality they have created onstage; a vocalization of the physical expression of the scene; verbal extension of the involvement and relationship between players; verbalization growing organically out of the life of a scene.

Dignity: Being oneself at any age; the acceptance of a person without trying to alter him or her.

Direct Experience: A space where individual equipment is awake and alive to what is going on; your whole self attentive; a space for intuition to emerge to assist in the ongoing event.

Dramatic Play: Acting out and/or living through old (or someone else's) real-life situations to find out how to fit within them; common play among nursery-school children attempting to become that which they fear, admire, or don't understand; identifying with characters in film, stage, and literature; living the character; not usable for the stage.

Egocentric: Fear of no support from others or from the environment; mistaken self-protection.

Emerge: Appearing from the invisible; becoming visible; to come forth; revelation.

Emote: Imposing self on audience; role-playing instead of playing a role.

Emotion: Organic motion created by the playing. Subjective emotion carried to the stage is not communication.

Energy: Level of intensity with which one approaches the problem; the inspiration released when a problem is solved; the power held bound in resistance to solving a problem; the power released in "explosion" (spontaneity); diagnostic action; the result of process (playing); contact.

Environment: The conditioned stage life agreed upon by members of the group; all the animate and inanimate objects within the theater, including self and the audience; an explorable place.

Equality: Not to be confused with sameness; the right of everyone of any age or background to become part of the theater community, enter into its activities, view its problems, work on them; the right to gain knowledge; the right to knock on any door.

Evaluation: Method of criticism through involvement with the problem rather than each other.

Exposure: Seeing or being seen directly, not as others would like you or themselves to be.

Feeling: Private to the actor; not for public viewing; feeling between players onstage must become the object between them; belongs to sensory equipment.

Floor Plan: A drawing or a plan (on paper or on a blackboard) of the structure for an acting problem: Where (the objects), Who (the actors), What (the activity), focus (the problem); a layout of the Where agreed upon and drawn up by a group of players; the "field" upon which the "game" will be played; a map of the territory the players must enter into and explore; ground plan.

Focus: Directed viewing to keep you in process. An anchor (stability) which makes movement possible.

Frame of Reference: A referral of point on which judgments are made; a referral point from which one views the world; a reference conditioned (framed) by cultural, familial, and educational patterns.

Game: An accepted group activity which is limited by rules and group agreement; fun, spontaneity, enthusiasm, and joy accompany games;

parallels the theater experience; a set of rules that keeps a player playing.

Generalization: Occluded sensory perception; refusal to "give life to the object"; assuming others know what you are trying to communicate.

Ghostly Voices: The past; emotional dependency on rules of behavior subtly and unconsciously (for the most part) interwoven into our own voices, psyche, and gestures by parents, teachers, spouses, institutions, employers, dictators, and culture. The proper and improper ways of behaving—"You can't do that!" "Use the other fork!" "Did you wash your hands?" "Be nice!" "Don't embarrass me!" "That's a good baby!" The ghostly voices intrude, invade, color, distort, interrupt, permeate, even corrupt any ongoing event, making direct experience impossible.

Gibberish: Meaningless sounds substituted for recognizable words that force the players to communicate by physicalizing (showing); an acting exercise.

Good Taste: Allowing something its own character without imposing anything alien upon it; adding nothing to detract from itself; a sense of the inherent nature of an object, scene, or character; it is one's recognition of the nature of something.

Group: A community of interests; individuals freely gathering around a project to explore, build, use, or alter it.

Group Agreement: Group decision; agreed reality between players; agreed reality between players and audience; acceptance of the rules of the game; group agreement on focus; we cannot play without group agreement; breaks tie to teacher-director.

Heightening: Intensifying a relationship, a character, or a scene onstage; creating a high level of reality; giving a greater dimension to life reality; underlining life; enlargement of character or event for clarity in communicating to the audience; to make a point through heightening; using anything or everything (acting, technical, or verbal) to make an impact.

How: Preplanning How keeps the intuitive from working by plotting a situation as opposed to meeting whatever comes up at the moment of playing; preparing oneself for every move as opposed to waiting to see what will happen; fear of venturing out into the unknown; giving examples of ways of solving the problem; performing.

Illusion: The theater is not illusion; it is a reality agreed upon by the group and understood by the audience; subjective projection.

Imagination: Subjective; inventive; creating one's own ideas of how things should be; playing in the theater requires *group* creation as opposed to individually creating one's own idea of how things should be; belonging to the intellect as opposed to coming from the intuitive.

Improvisation: Playing the game; setting out to solve a problem with no preconception about how you will do it; permitting everything in the environment (animate or inanimate) to work for you in solving the problem. It is not the scene, it is the way to the scene; a predominate function of the intuitive. Playing the game brings opportunity to learn theater to a cross-section of people. "Playing it by ear"; process as opposed to result; not ad-lib or originality or making it up by yourself; a form, if understood, possible to any age group; setting object in motion between players as in a game; solving of problems together; the ability to allow the acting problem to evolve the scene; a moment in the lives of people without needing a plot or story line for the communication; an art form; transformation; brings forth details and relationships as organic whole; living process.

Improvised Play: A scene or play developed from improvisation used for performance; group-created material; a scene or play developed from situation or scenario; play or scene evolving out of the group playing; not a "story conference."

Inner Action: Recognizing an emotion through sensory response; use of inner action allows player the privacy of personal feelings (emotion); using emotion as an object; "Physicalize that feeling!"

Inner Voice: Your real (higher?) self, viewing objectively, recommending side-coaching moves.

Insight: A moment of revelation; seeing that which was there all the time; knowing:

> The tree was a tree
> Before you could see
> The tree.

Inspiration: Energy fortified with intuitive knowledge.

Intellect: The computer, collector of information, facts, statistics, data of all kinds; should not function separately; part of an organic whole.

Interpretation: Giving one's frame of reference as opposed to directly relating to events; adding or subtracting from a direct communication; might cause inability to meet a fresh moment of experience.

Intruding: Telling how to solve the problem; showing actors how to walk, talk, emote, feel, and read lines; meddling; inability to play.

Intuitive: The x-area; an area to be prodded and investigated by everyone; unhampered knowledge beyond the sensory equipment (physical and mental); the area of revelation.

Invent: Rearrangement of known phenomena limited by personal reality; from the intellect; solo playing.

Involvement: Earnestly entering into the game or exercise; playing. Discipline is involvement; involvement with object creates release and freedom to relate.

Judging: Playing safe; everything viewed going through your past prejudices; no chance for spontaneous action.

Judgment: Subjective placement of good/bad, right/wrong based on old frames of reference, cultural or family patterns (personal) rather than a fresh response to a moment of experiencing; imposition.

Labels: Terms which tend to obscure their origin and block organic knowledge. The use of labels limits one to things and categories and neglects relationships.

Learned Response: A reaction rather than an action; keeps players from moving out into the environment; keeps players from exploration and self-discovery; a shut door; "That's no way to do it!" "Why?" "My teacher said so!"

Learning: The capacity for experiencing.

Manipulation: Using problem, fellow actors, etc., for egocentric purposes; being opportunistic; manifests itself by resisting relating to fellow players.

Mind: Part of the body; flows through the physical brain.

Multiple Stimuli: The many things coming out of the environment at the player which he or she must be aware of and act upon.

No Motion: A series of stills (steps) that create movement; an exercise in which movement is broken down into held parts and then reassembled back into movement; an exercise which shows students that since present movement includes past time, they need not dwell on the past; can be used to heighten time; gives insight into compulsive action; helps student to see his or her present (onstage) environment and make contact with himself or herself within it.

Nonacting: Involving oneself with a focus; detachment; a working approach to all the problems of the theater; keeping one's personal feelings private;

learning to act through nonacting; showing, not
telling; "Stop acting!"

Nondirectional Blocking: Sharing the stage picture; self-blocking without outside direction;
developing the skill to see the stage (outward) picture while inside it; group assistance from fellow
players in blocking; necessary technique for the
actor in improvisational theater; player's skill in
evolving stage movement from the progressing
scene; a way to self-identify; helps break dependency on teacher-director.

Nonverbal: Teaching without lectures on techniques for the actor; language used only to present
and clarify or evaluate a problem; not telling the student How to solve a problem; not spelling it out;
breaks dependency on the teacher-director; nonverbal system of teaching as used in this handbook;
another form of communication between players.

Object: Object and focus may be used inter-
changeably; sets the actor in motion; used for playing, as a ball, between players; involvement with
object makes relationship between players possible; mutual focus on an outside reality (the rope
between players); a technique to keep actors from
subjective response; meditation; a mutual problem
allowing freedom of personal expression in solving
it; the springboard into the intuitive; the physical-

ization of an agreed object, feeling, or event out of which a scene evolves.

Objective: Anything outside a person; to be objective; the ability to allow an outside phenomenon its own character and life; not changing what is to suit subjective assumptions; being objective is basic to improvisational theater.

Objective Reality: That which can be seen and used between players; created by group agreement; a means of sharing our humanness; a changing theater reality that springs from group agreement.

Occupation: The stage activity; that which is created by the actors and visible to the audience; that which the audience shares with the audience; the What.

Off-balance Moment: The gateway to the intuition; the moment when in full sensory attention, you don't think, you act!

Organic: A head-to-foot response where mind (intellect), body, and intuition function as one unit; in one piece; part of everything, of itself; out of itself; functioning out of total humanness.

Pantomime: An art form related to the dance; not to be confused with "silent scenes" or a "scene without words."

Pause: Seeing what is happening right now! Time and space are given a moment.

Perception: Knowing without use of the intellect alone; osmosis; awareness of outside phenomena; ability to reach out into the environment; to become the object; intuition; x-area.

Performance: Not to be confused with exhibitionism; letting go; a moment of surrender creating harmony and refreshment; a moment of personal freedom.

Personal Freedom: One's own nature; not mirroring others; an expression of self free of authoritarian (approval/disapproval) needs; freedom to accept or reject rules of the game; recognition of limitation and freedom to reject or accept it; not to be confused with license; freedom from emotionalism; a moment of reality in which one has a part in the construction; freedom from survival clothes; a private matter.

Perspective: Looking into; an objective view; detachment; the long view.

Physicalization: Showing and not telling; a physical manifestation of a communication; a physical expression of an attitude; using self to put an object in motion; giving life to the object; "Physicalize that feeling!" "Physicalize that relationship!"

"Physicalize that pinball machine, kite, fish, object, taste!," etc.

Player: One who plays; person skilled in creating the theatrical reality; pulling rabbits out of a hat; an actor; a nonacting actor.

Playing: Fun, enjoyment, enthusiasm, trust; heightening the object; moving relations with fellow players; involvement with the focus; the physical expression of the life force; a term usable instead of rehearsal in improvisational theater; "Let's play!"

Playing a Role: Playing as in a game; playing a role and not subjective playing of self; sharing a characterization and not using a character for emotional outbursts; keeping self-identity.

Playwriting: Manipulation of situation and fellow actors; an unwillingness to believe that a scene will evolve out of the group playing; not understanding the focus; deliberately using old action, dialogue, information, and facts (ad-libbing) instead of spontaneous selection during improvisation; not usable in improvisational theater; "Stop playwriting!"

Point of Concentration: A chosen agreed object (or event) on which to focus; a technique to achieve detachment; the object around which the players gather; involvement with focus brings relationships; "Trust the focus!"; a vehicle that transports the player. It opens the student-audience to receive the communication; preoccupation.

Preoccupation: The energy source; that which is not visible to the audience. By creating two-way problems, preoccupation eliminates the watcher and thus makes playing possible.

Preplanning: Planning how to work a scene as opposed to just letting it happen; related to playwriting; a mental rehearsal; the uncertain child. Preplanning is to be used only for structure.

Pretend: Substitution for reality; subjective as opposed to real (objective); "If you pretend, it isn't real"; imposing self on a problem as opposed to creating reality; thinking about an object's reality instead of giving it reality; improvisational theater grows out of objective reality; not accepting *any* reality.

Problem: That which involves you in the moment; a problem prefigures a solution.

Problem Solving: A system of learning theater techniques through solving of problems as opposed to intellectualizing and verbalizing; puts player(s) into action (physicalizes); does away with preplanning; presents a simple operational structure (as in a game) so that anyone can play.

Process: The doing; process is goal, and goal is endless process; there can be no final statement on a character, relationship, scene, system of work.

Psychodrama: Putting one's own emotion into play to create action; living story instead of in process.

React: Withdrawal; self-protection; response to another's act as opposed to self-acting; attacking to avoid changing position; making thrust into the environment instead of moving out into it; fear of acting; fear of taking responsibility for an action.

Recall: Subjective memory (dead); deliberately bringing back a personal, private, past life-experience to get an emotional or character quality; confused by many with acting. To use past experience, deliberately evoked for a present-time problem, is clinical and can be destructive to the theater reality and artistic detachment. In spontaneous selection, the intuitive gives us past experiences organically as part of a total life process. Can be used by a director as a *device* (when nothing else works) for getting a mood or quality; bringing back a past memory through manipulation; related to psychodrama.

Relationship: Contact with fellow players; playing; a mutual involvement with an object. Relationship grows out of object-involvement, allows players the privacy of personal feeling while playing together, prevents intrusion or meddling.

Resistance: Manipulation of Where, Who, What; unwillingness to understand and/or explore the focus; indicated by jokes, playwriting, clowning, withdrawal, acting; fear of changing in any way. Resistance is held or bottled-up energy; when resistance is broken, a new experience takes place.

Respect: Recognition of another; to *know* one another.

Rigidity: Held in; inability to alter one's point of view; inability to see another's point of view; armored against contact with others; armored against ideas other than one's own; fear of contact.

Rocking the Boat: Unbalanced stage; refers to self-blocking; "You're rocking the boat!"; a term for very young actors in teaching them self-blocking.

Role-playing: As opposed to playing a role; imposing a character as opposed to creating a role out of the problem; psychodrama; dramatic play; artificial imposition of character on self as opposed to allowing natural growth to evolve out of relationship; subjective response to "what is a character"; using a character to hide behind; a mask keeping one from exposure; withdrawal; solo performance.

Rules of the Game: Includes the structure (Where, Who, and What) and the object (focus) plus group agreement.

Scene: An event that grows out of the focus; the results of playing; a fragment; a moment in the lives of people needing no beginning, middle, or end, biography or statistics; the scene is the game coming out of the rules; playing is the process out of which the scene evolves by involvement with an object (focus) and relationship with fellow players.

Seasoning the Actor: Integrating all parts of the whole (theater techniques, playing, showing, etc.); releasing ability to meet all crises with certainty; making oneself comfortable in the stage environment.

Seeing: Seeing (objective) as opposed to believing (subjective); a term used as opposed to imagining or pretending; "See it!"; part of the sensory equipment; to see so you can show; to let the audience see a play as in a game; skillful playing; to look; looking at the phenomenal world and *seeing* it; seeing as opposed to staring; looking and seeing as opposed to pretending to look and thus staring; "If you see it, we (the audience) see it!"

Seeing the Word: The physical reality of consonants and vowels; the visualization brought up by a word; a sensory contact with words; the design and shape of sounds.

Self: Refers to the natural part of ourselves; free of crippling mores, prejudices, rote information, and static frames of reference; that part of us capable of direct contact with the environment; that which is our own nature; the part of ourselves that functions free of the need for approval/disapproval; cutting through makeup, costume, rags, mannerisms, character, junk jewelry, etc., that make up the covering (survival clothes) of self. Self must be found before one can play; playing helps find self. Right brain; x-area.

Self-identity: Having one's own place and allowing others theirs; securely placed within an environment. Where you are is where *you* are.

Sensory: Body and mind; to see, taste, hear, feel, think, perceive; to know through the physical as opposed to the intuitive.

Set Pieces: Random furniture, blocks, props used to make the Where.

Share with Your Audience: Brings harmony and relationship between players and audience; making audience part of the game; used in side coaching to develop self-blocking; the same as rocking the boat used for very young actors; "Share your voice!" "Share the stage picture!" Share yourself!"; used from the first workshop to accomplish self-blocking and voice projection; removes need for labels; develops ability to see the outside view of the stage while inside of it.

Showing: Physicalizing objects, involvements, and relationships as opposed to verbalizing (telling); spontaneous experience. The actor brings creation or invention into the phenomenal world by *showing;* physicalizing.

Side Coaching: Assistance that takes responsibility for guiding you through a problem and keeps you on focus whenever you have lost it, making you, yourself, an objective viewer. "Out of your head and into the space!"

Sight Lines: The clarity of vision of an *individual* in the audience to every single *individual* at work onstage.

Situation: A Where, Who, What, and Why which becomes the structure for a scene; the framework (skeleton play) in which problem is placed. The situation is not the problem.

Skeleton Play: A set form for which improvisation is used; a scenario; a way of building an improvised play; a series of beats/scenes which must be filled in by the players.

Space: Something about which we know very little; the stage area where a reality can be placed; space can be used to shape the realities we create; an area of no boundaries; without limits; the player uses space to bring reality into the phenomenal world; to make space for the object; the larger environment; the space beyond; a place to perceive or receive a communication.

Spontaneity: A moment of explosion; a free moment of self-expression; an off-balance moment; the gateway to your intuition; the moment when, in full sensory attention, you don't think, you *act!*

Spontaneous: Entering the off-balance moment; facing the unknown and uncharted unafraid, free of the ghostly voices.

Spontaneous Selection: Selecting that which is appropriate to the problem without calculation; a spontaneous choice of alternatives at a moment of crisis; since theater is a series of crises, spontaneous selection should be working all the time; selecting out of the "explosion" that which is *immediately* useful; insight.

Stage Business: A stage activity used to implement, accent, intensify, or heighten; the manner in which one plays the objects in the environment; the way the "ball" is kept bouncing; stage business grows out of involvement with objects and relationship with fellow actors. Gibberish exercises are especially useful regarding this point.

Stage Fright: The fear of disapproval or indifference; separation of audience and actors, placing audience as viewers or judges; fear of exposure; when audience is "part of the game," stage fright leaves.

Staring: A curtain in front of the eyes to prevent contact with others; playing for oneself only; a self-protective wall; "See us!"

Static: A held moment having what has happened and what will and/or may happen within it; crises.

Statistics: Giving audience and fellow players facts, information, and/or biographies about each other; telling, not showing; expressing a character verbally; using facts, past information, etc., instead of improvising and letting the character come forth; "No facts, no information, no biographies. Show us!"

Story: A story is an epitaph; the ashes of the fire; story is the result (residue) of a process; improvisational theater is process; for story (play) to live, it must be broken down into its separate parts or beats (disassembled) to become process again; a well-written play is process.

Structure: The Where, Who, and What; the field on which the game is played.

Student's Progress: Any distance a person has traveled from his or her starting point.

Subjective: Self-involved; inability to contact the environment and let it show itself; difficulty in playing with others; defensiveness which makes it difficult to understand how to play the game.

Subjectivity: Inability to see a tree as a tree, filling every space with "me, me, me."

Suggestions by the Audience: A primitive audience involvement; overtly making audience part of the game.

Survival Clothes: Behaviorisms, mannerisms, dress, IQ, affectations, makeup, personality traits, frames of reference, prejudices, body distortions, opportunism used to protect ourselves in living; must be seen for what they are to be freed for the learning process; status.

Teacher-director: Teacher works for the students (unblocking, etc.), director works for the overall stage; presents problems for both the individual experience and the stage experience.

Telling: Verbalizing the involvements, Where, etc., of a situation rather than creating a reality and showing or allowing the scene to emerge through physical attitudes, relationships, etc.; inaction; nonplaying; results of telling are ad-libbing, playwriting, manipulation; imposing self on object, not letting object move self; "acting."

Theater Reality: Agreed reality; any reality the players choose to create; total freedom in creating a reality; giving life to a created reality; allowing space for a created reality.

Theme: The moving thread (life) that weaves itself into every beat of the play and unifies all the elements in the production.

Timing: Ability to handle the multiple stimuli going on within the theater activity.

Transformation: Creation; momentarily breaks through isolation, and actors and audience alike receive (ahhh!) the appearance of a new reality (theater magic); improvisation.

Trusting the Scheme: Letting go and giving oneself to playing.

Two-way Problem: Gives focus to the intellect and thus preoccupies the actor to remove any inhibiting or censoring mechanisms that keep one from playing; blanks the mind; "I didn't know what I was saying"; preoccupation/occupation; releases intuitive levels of new energy.

Verbalization: Players telling the audience about the Where and the character relationships rather than showing; teacher-director giving *his or her* knowledge to the student; excessive verbalization of subject matter; suggests egocentricity and/or exhibitionism; excessive verbalization on the part of student-actor is mistrust of self-ability to show; a cover-up; teaching through words as opposed to allowing student-actor to experience; teaching swimming verbally without allowing anyone in the water.

Visualization (Image): The deliberate use of an existing form (animate or inanimate) to aid in creating a character or a dramatic moment; evoking stimuli for a character or feeling through a device outside of the scene involvement. Not recommended.

Watcher: A constant eye upon us; a restrictive control; one who judges; approval/disapproval. Fear of the eye keeps self hidden from fresh experience and brings forth a dummy self through posturing, delinquency, apathy, stupidity, wordiness; "a watched pot never boils."

What: Your activity; what you are doing.

Where: You are there, in your setting and/or environment.

Who: Your character and/or relationship, shown by behavior toward another rather than by telling.

Words: Gibberish; chatter; verbalizing for lack of action; "Just words!"; playwriting; words as opposed to dialogue; words "in place of"; keep self hidden.

X-area: See "Intuitive."

GLOSSARY OF
SIDE-COACHING PHRASES

All side coaching* is given/received during playing and rehearsal. As side coach you are not a director, separate and apart, but stand *within focus and involvement* on the rule. As player, you do not stop to consider what is being side coached, you *act!* When side coaching begins to work for you, a symbiotic connection between you and your focus results.

Your role as side coach is also to keep yourself playing, whatever that may necessitate, when playing has stopped and you have become fragmented. Side coaching excites you to action and hurtles you into the present.

Every game has its own side coaching, not all included in the phrases which follow. The glossary is intended to help you develop the ability to coach yourself freely in many different circumstances.

---

* See also "Side Coaching Yourself," page 7, and "Suggested Games for Specific Needs," page 123.

Act! Don't react! Act goes forward; *react* is internalized before going out.

Allow the focus to work for you! Should *relax* player. Helps release obsessive control. An *outside force* is working and helping.

Camera! Head-to-toe camera on ———*!* Putting full focus and energy on another player.

Contact! Vowels and consonants! Attitude! Spell! Reminders.

Expand that gesture! Pause! Widens experience.

Expand that object! Idea! Sound! Thought! Puts you into a meditative observation as exploration is sought.

Extend the sound! Reinforces movement, sight, thought, character.

Feel that! In your back! Feet! Head! Shoulders! An emotion takes over the whole body.

Follow the follower! You *reflect* without initiating.

Give! Take! Take! Give! Awareness of others.

Give the ball (the word, the pause, the look) its time and space! A pause is given. Time/space can be a very emotional stage moment.

Heighten that moment . . . that feeling! Brings a brighter, broader, intensified experience.

Help your fellow player who isn't playing! Awakens cast to others' needs. Produces much stage business.

Keep your eye on the ball! Your fellow player! Your prop! Anchors you in movement.

Let the space support you! Don't worry about what that means. Your body will understand.

Let your sight flow through your eyes! Let the sound flow through your ears! Let your mind flow through your brain! Useful for SPACE WALKS.

No Motion! Stops excessive head control. Puts action and thought on a back burner. Puts the focus of a game in No Motion.

No Motion on the inner dialogue! A waiting (not waiting for, but *in* waiting). Peripheral thought, ambivalent thought, is nowhere to be found.

No playwriting! No acting! Reminds one to get "out of the head" and "into the space!"

No urgency! Helps you get "out of the head."

Occlude your fellow player! Occlude the Where! Occlude the audience! Gives a new relation with the occluded; adds sight by bringing the occluded into sharp focus, as in a closeup; keeps a player from hiding. Can bring out hidden character qualities.

Out of your head, into the space! Open for the communication! Useful to get rid of attitudes. You move out into the stage space. Frees the intuition (x-area).

Pause! Opens the possibility of a direct experience. Time and space are given a moment onstage.

Penetrate! Extends your sensory equipment.

Physicalize that thought! Gives physical (body) expression to a budding, emerging emotion.

Reflect! Don't initiate! To reflect is to include another; to initiate is to deny yourself.

Release! Your attitudes, your muscle-holds!

See! Allow yourself to be seen! Come out, come out, wherever you are.

See in Slow Motion! You see and feel what is going on.

See the ceiling! The walls! Look out the window! Awakens you to the Where.

See unlabeled! Fresh sight is called upon.

See with your whole body! As if standing on tiptoe.

Share the space between you! Meet in the middle. The between space is where the individual energies can meet. Produces artistic detachment, makes apparent to the players what is happening in regard to character and emotion.

Share your voice! Produces projection, responsibility to the audience. Not simply a direction to speak louder; it helps to alert one organically, without the need for a lecture, to the need for personal interaction with the audience.

Slow Motion! Brings you into the moment of your playing. Details become sharpened.

Stage picture! Helps you to see audience view. Brings you and audience into the stage space.

Stage whisper! Reminds you to whisper audibly. Intensifies relationships.

Stay out of it! Stops interfering. Stops controls.

Take a ride on your own body! View the scenery! Creates great artistic detachment.

Touch! Allow yourself to be touched! Expands the sensual world.

Use your whole body! Helps to physicalize emotions, feelings, thoughts, character.

You name it! You supply your own side coaching.

ALPHABETICAL LIST OF GAMES

ABOUT THE AUTHOR

VIOLA SPOLIN, the originator of theater games, was introduced to the use of games, storytelling, folk dance, and dramatics as tools for stimulating creative expression in the 1920s while a student of Neva Boyd at Chicago's Hull House. During her years as a teacher and supervisor of creative dramatics there, she began to develop her nonverbal, nonpsychological approach. Her books have been translated into Swedish, German, and Portuguese. She died in 1994.